WHITE BOY BLACK GIRL

WHITE BOY BLACK GIRL

WHAT OUR DIFFERENCES CAN TEACH US, ONE HONEST CONVERSATION AT A TIME

ADAEZE & CHAD BRINKMAN

TYNDALE
MOMENTUM®

A Tyndale nonfiction imprint

Visit Tyndale online at tyndale.com.

Visit Tyndale Momentum online at tyndalemomentum.com.

Tyndale, Tyndale's quill logo, *Tyndale Momentum,* and the *Tyndale Momentum* logo are registered trademarks of Tyndale House Ministries. Tyndale Momentum is a nonfiction imprint of Tyndale House Publishers, Carol Stream, Illinois.

Designed by Lindsey Bergsma

Published in association with the literary agency of Gardner Literary LLC. www.gardner-literary.com.

For information about special discounts for bulk purchases, please contact Tyndale House Publishers at csresponse@tyndale.com, or call 1-855-277-9400.

Library of Congress Cataloging-in-Publication Data

A catalog record for this book is available from the Library of Congress.

ISBN 978-1-4964-7493-3

Printed in the United States of America

30	29	28	27	26	25	24
7	6	5	4	3	2	1

Holy Spirit, come make the soil
of our story on these pages
fertile ground for Your work to be done.
In Jesus' Name, amen.

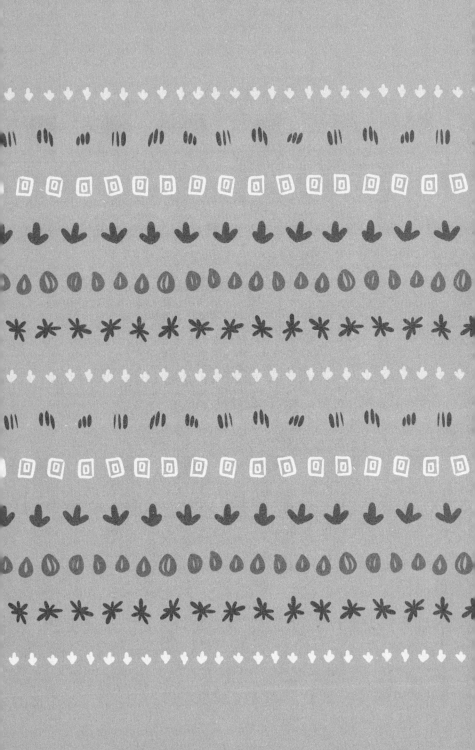

CONTENTS

WELCOME TO OUR WORLD!

Ey, errybody! We're Chadaeze. Welcome to us. *Lip pop from Adaeze.*

Hopefully, it goes without saying that *Chadaeze* is short for Chad and Adaeze (Nigerian pronunciation: "ah-DEH-zeh"; American inflection: "uh-DAY-zee," like the flower). That's our couple name, because we a couple, and we creative like that.

Thanks for picking up our book! We're humbled and honored to have the opportunity to share part of our story with you.

When our relationship first started, we both brought a lot of baggage with us. We were two very different people from two very different backgrounds—a white man with a good heart and good intentions but a lot of cultural blind spots and a family history of strong racial bias, and a Black woman dealing with the sting of years of cultural misunderstanding and racial microaggressions that resulted in some pretty significant trust issues.

We both had a lot to learn, and we both needed to give each other a bit of grace because the experiences we had prior to meeting gave us lenses that colored every conversation we had and triggered a lot of strong emotions. This is exactly why racial topics are so difficult to broach. They are, by their very nature, intensely personal.

Even though we're coming at this from the perspective of our crazy-about-each-other marriage, this book is not just for married people or people in romantic relationships. It's for everyone. And we think you'll find that the vast majority of what we talk about is just as applicable to relationships with your friends from church, your neighbors, and your coworkers.

You'll quickly discover that we're not perfect, but because we love and trust each other, we have the freedom to speak openly about some pretty sensitive topics that aren't the norm in most relationships.

We offer two often-different perspectives from two always-different people who are complete societal opposites and who love and enjoy each other deeply. This book is a record of how we've done things. And whether we got things right or just flat-out stepped in it, we hope our journey will help empower you on your journey—or, at the very least, help you avoid some of the potholes and point out some of the sights you don't wanna miss along the way.

Our goal is to provide you with a safe space to eavesdrop on some of the more difficult conversations we've had about race with each other, our friends, and our families so you can learn how to navigate similar conversations in a way that's honoring and respect-ful to both parties and gain a deeper understanding of yourself and others.

So we'd like to invite you into the middle. The middle of the discomfort. The middle of the tension. The middle of asking, "How do I . . . ?"

Stay with us.

We believe on the other side of that uneasy middle is unity where there has long been division, healing where there has long been trauma, and reconciliation where there has long been opposition.

We're guessing you're here because you wanna be a better friend, coworker, neighbor, and basically all-around human being in a multicultural context. That's awesome! We hope this book will encourage you to enter into some of those tough conversations you've been wanting to have with your friends and coworkers across racial lines but weren't quite sure how or where to start.

Fair warning: things get deep. During our writing process, there were moments when it was difficult to put words to paper. That's just the reality of talking about the effect racism has on the world. It's difficult. We have all been taught and accepted certain things as truth based on our own experiences, and unfortunately, a lot of what we've come to accept as "normal" is actually quite hurtful. If we're gonna come together, we have to be willing to reevaluate some of our preconceived notions and look at the world through a different lens. That's what this book is all about. At times, it will be tough, but trust us when we say the effort will be worth it—and some of the resulting relationships could become the most meaningful ones in your life.

As you read, you may feel uncomfortable, challenged, or possibly even attacked at times. Believe it or not, that's a good thing! Some of what you read on these pages *should* hit a nerve. It means you're identifying an area where you need to start seeing or thinking about things a little differently. We know how hard it can be to hold a mirror up to ourselves. Let's face it: we don't always like what we see. But we also know firsthand the blessing of having our eyes opened to our blind spots. You know, the ones that turn a well-intentioned comment or question into a panicked retreat of "Noooo, that's not what I meant!" and leave us scrambling to explain, hoping the other person hasn't already tapped out of the conversation or, worse, the relationship.

So, if something you read gives you a check in your spirit, pay attention. Lean into it. Ask yourself where it's coming from and why it's making you feel uncomfortable or defensive. And please, know our goal here isn't to make anyone feel guilty or to shut anyone down. In fact, it's just the opposite. Our goal is to tear down the walls that decades of racial tension have built between people, help us learn about one another, and celebrate what makes us all unique. All we ask is that you keep an open mind and be willing to consider—and hopefully even embrace—a slightly different perspective.

And if something we talk about hits a little too close to home and you end up throwing this book across the room, that's cool. We get it. We've been there. But we've also managed to work our way through the sludge and muck, and by God's grace, we've emerged with more humility, more strength, and more closeness than before.

So go ahead—freak out. If you have to, walk away from the book for a while. It's okay. When you come back, we'll still be sitting here by the fire with a glass of whiskey, ready to pick up wherever you left off.

Last, but most importantly, you should know that we love Jesus, and we boldly approach the conversations ahead from that perspective. If you don't share our faith, we encourage you not to check out right here. This book is for everyone, and there is still a lot you can learn from someone who sees the world differently from you. (Kinda what we tryna get at in this book, if you haven't noticed.)

All through the writing process, we've prayed for our hearts to align with God's heart for this message. We pray that as you read, our words will ooze the grace and truth of Jesus, and that together we can allow a little bit of the peace and unity of heaven to invade the earth.

THE FIVE WORDS
THAT CHANGED EVERYTHING

❦ ❦ ❦ ❦ ❦ ❦ ❦ ❦ ❦ ❦ ❦ ❦ ❦ ❦ ❦ ❦ ❦

A: It was a cool November afternoon, and I was getting ready to go on a date with my newly official (as of a month prior) boyfriend, Chad.

We were going to have lunch at a brewery (his idea). Chad had been steadily passing his extensive beer knowledge along to me, and to his delight, it was starting to rub off—even though I still made a bitter-beer face whenever I tried his favorite IPAs. I honestly didn't care where we went—I was just excited to hang out with my favorite person. Give me all the chill time with my bearded man as he drinks a beer like his mountain-man sexy self do.

I was going for a comfy I'ma-look-geuh casual look, so with Beyoncé's "Brown Skin Girl" soundtracking my getting-ready process, I put on some light makeup and threw on a quirky T-shirt that read PIZZA IS MY BAE, some high-waisted jeans, and a multicolored scarf from Zara that I styled to resemble an ichafu on my head.

As the only Black person on a staff of over 150 people, I had recently reembraced the boldness of expressing myself, and part of that was not being ashamed to represent my Nigerian heritage in creative ways. Having been told more than once that I was "too much" and "probably unattractive" to most white guys in Colorado because they didn't grow up around Black women, the fact that I felt so comfortable being myself with Chad seemed like an act of God.

Chad wasn't like other guys in my sparse dating history. I never had to wonder where we stood, what his level of interest was, or how he felt about me, and we helped free each other to be our full selves. Plus, by this point, we'd both had enough dating experience to know that ain't nobody got time to fake who we are. We both had an "Either you can accept me as *fully* me, or *bye*" mindset.

I always knew that the right guy for me wouldn't be intimidated by me but would also be able to handle me, and Chad had effortlessly proven that he was man enough to do both, as well as look to Jesus for how to care for my heart.

Feeling good, light, and not nervous at all, I grabbed a cardigan in case it got chilly later and skipped out the door.

C: When I saw the notification on my phone that Adaeze was on her way, my heart skipped a beat. We had hit the ground running in our relationship, and every time we saw each other, I wanted more. This day was no exception.

Now, I am a typical guy with four T-shirts, one pair of blue jeans (on which, to Adaeze's despair, I wipe my hands constantly), and a pair of bright red Vans I thought were the coolest thing ever (though I found out later that Adaeze was not a fan). That night I was going to proudly show off the Pacific Northwesterner I was, so I put on my hooded flannel jacket that matched my Vans and a plain T-shirt. I was going for cool and casual, but in reality, I couldn't calm the butterflies in my stomach.

When my phone pinged to tell me that Adaeze was close, I jumped up off the couch and ran to the front door, my inner monologue matching me step-for-step the entire way.

Just be cool.

Everything's gonna be great.

Why am I so nervous?

You're fine, she likes you.

Are you sure she likes you?

Of course she likes you.

Stop freaking yourself out.

Just calm down.

Breathe.

Don't be weird.

The second she rang the bell, I reached for the knob, then I hesitated. After all, I didn't want to look like I was just standing at the door waiting for her. *Just be cool . . .*

A: After several seconds, Chad swung open the door, and in what had become our traditional greeting, I bounded into his arms and wrapped my legs around him in an affectionate squeeze.

He grinned at me and asked, "You ready?"

"Yeh!" I eagerly responded. He grabbed his car keys, and I happily danced down his front steps, pausing at the bottom to wait for him. I held my hand out, and without breaking stride, he brought his hand down in a low-five-like slap, linking his fingers with mine.

As we drove to the brewery, we each talked about our day, my hand resting on top of his on the stick shift. When we arrived,

I asked if we could take a photo in the parking lot before going in. It was such a beautiful day, and okay, I'll admit it . . . the afternoon light was affirmatively agreeing with my melanin pop pop. Plus, Chad looked great, and we was cute together!

C: It was *not* a flattering photo of me. Honestly, I looked drunk. However, like all self-respecting men, the second the girl I liked asked me to take a picture, I happily obliged. Several slightly less inebriated looking selfies later, we headed into the brewery, where we were immediately seated at a booth on the main level of the restaurant.

The server came over to the table, greeted us, and asked if we would like anything to drink. Since I didn't know if Adaeze was aware of the difference between a sour and a pale ale yet, I graciously offered to help her choose a beer.

A: I knew what a sour was!

C: Okay . . . she knew what a sour was. We decided to order a flight. Adaeze picked a few mild beers, and I picked the rest to push her a little and see her bitter-hop face once or twice.

As soon as we gave our drink order, we got lost in conversation. The poor server came back three times before we even remembered to look at the menu. We were just perfectly content spending time together, talking, and holding hands. As far as I was concerned, we were the only two people in the room.

A: I was well aware of the rest of the room from the moment we sat down. I couldn't see everyone in the restaurant from where we were sitting, but as far as I could tell, I was the only Black person in the room.

This is something I'd grown to be more aware of that year, in the midst of all the racial unrest. Also, we were seated in a booth next to the entrance and close to the restrooms, which meant everyone coming in and leaving saw us, as did everyone going to the restroom. The looks as people passed our booth were hard to miss.

Focus on Chad, I thought. *Don't let this ruin the fun you're having together.* I squeezed Chad's hand tighter, leaned forward a bit, and zeroed in on his eyes. He did the same.

C: *I wonder what she's thinking about . . .*

A: *I wonder what he's thinking about . . .*

C: *Man, she's looking good tonight.*

A: *Maybe they're not even looking at us. Maybe they're looking at the picture behind us.*

C: *How did I end up sitting across the table from this girl? What did I do that God would put me here with her?*

A: *Maybe they're looking at us because we're a beautiful couple.*

C: *I bet I could turn her into a Seahawks fan.*

A: *Okay, seriously, if that old lady looks over here one more time . . .*

C: *I could go anywhere with her and have a great time.*

A: *Should I say something to him about the looks?*

A: I couldn't tell if Chad had noticed the looks or not. If he hadn't, I wasn't sure I wanted to bring it up. Whenever I raised questions about race at work, I always felt like "that Black girl" who kept "bringing it up" or "making everything about race." I didn't want to be that Black girl today. Not here. Not with Chad. Then, shortly after our food arrived, it happened. There was an older white woman who kept looking at us. To do so, she had to swivel around in her chair a full 180 degrees. It was blatant, and we both saw it.

C: "Umm, I feel like the woman to my right keeps looking at us."

A: "Yeah, and so is that woman over there . . . and that couple back there . . . and almost everyone who goes in and out of the restroom."

C: "Oh . . . I didn't notice."

A: *Huh.* I didn't want to punish Chad for not noticing, nor did I really know how to explain why this was bothering me without making him feel bad. "Soooo . . ." I began, tryna sound casual, "what do *you* think the looks mean?"

C: "Maybe they're not used to interracial couples?"

A: "Or maybe they're just admiring us because we look geuh . . . ?"

C: "Yeah, let's go with that." [awkward pause] "You okay?"

A: "Yeah. I just . . . don't like being stared at like that."

C: "What's making you feel uncomfortable?"

A: "Well . . . wouldn't you be bothered by a bunch of people staring at you?"

C: "Yeah, at times. Right now, I'm not feeling it too much though."

A: "Maybe that's because everyone in here looks like you."

C: "Oh . . ." Until this point in our relationship, nothing had made me feel uncomfortable being in white spaces together, but it was suddenly clear to me that Adaeze was far more aware of the white space than I was.

A: "Babe, no, no, no," I quickly reassured him. "I'm not trying to make you feel uncomfortable. It's all good." [Quick shift.] "How's your pulled pork sando?"

C: "No, wait, babe. I want to talk about this."

A: "Okay . . ." Chad and I had talked about race before, but this was the first time we had to talk about it specifically regarding *us*, in the present. For the first time, we were experiencing microaggressions toward us in public, in real time, together.

C: "I'll be honest . . . I don't really know what to ask." I really didn't.

A: "It's okay, babe, I gotchu." I sat back in my seat and gestured toward the room. "Do you understand the reality of us being together—here—in White-orado?"

C: "Yeah, I think so—I mean us being together is going to draw some looks and stuff."

A: "Yeah, but that has different implications for me than it does for you."

C: "We *are* different though. God made us different on purpose. Your culture made you into all that you are, and that's beautiful."

A: "Thank you. Buuuut . . . that's not the point." I didn't want to push too hard too soon, though I was relieved we were talking about it. I knew Chad well, but this was new territory in our relationship, and I was trying to get a pulse on how deep he was willing to go with me. "You don't feel uncomfortable in all-white spaces, and why would you? You're white. But it doesn't seem like you understand why *I* would feel uncomfortable when we get disapproving looks."

C: "So the reality of us being together is that we will have to deal with white people's disapproval . . . because they don't approve of you?"

A: "Yes." [Uncomfortable pause.] "So what does that mean for us?"

C: "That just means we're going to face stuff like this. Us being together will make people respond in ways that are frustrating, sure, but that doesn't bother me. I'll happily go anywhere with you." I so had this.

A: It felt like he was missing the point. The Band-Aid comment of "I'll be there" was fine, but I longed for Chad to take the next step in his awareness—not just being proud to be with me but also being aware of our different realities.

"Okay, but it still doesn't seem like you're understanding *why* the looks make me feel the way I feel."

C: "Racism?"

A: *For the love of God, finally, you freaking white man.* "Yes."

C: By now, I could see that Adaeze did not feel like I fully understood what she was trying to tell me. I wanted her to feel completely understood and supported and know that I was a safe space for her. I wanted to say something that would make her feel known, seen, and appreciated, so I said, "I feel like we are close . . ."

A: *Uh-huh.*

C: "And I understand . . ."

A: *Sure ya do.*

C: ". . . that the world looks at us differently. And with us being together, I am going to have to feel that with you a little bit."

A: *Yeah . . .*

C: "I am totally for you, and I want to support all of who you are, including what makes us different."

A: *Okay . . .*

C: "That's why I will still kiss you and hold your hand, even when you're wearing that!" I said, pointing at Adaeze's headwrap.

A: That definitely nicked something. I could tell his heart was trying to show through, though, so I decided to put a pin in it and come back to it later.

As we walked out to the car, Chad threw his arm around me, and I wrapped my arm around his waist. When we got into the car, I took another selfie of us, and as Chad pulled out of the parking lot, I looked at the photo on my phone with mixed emotions. *I really like this guy, but . . .*

C: Something was off. I had my hand on the stick shift, but this time, Adaeze didn't put her hand on mine, and she was much quieter than she had been on the ride out. I was totally confused. I mean, we had just succeeded in our first big conversation about race and what that meant for us as a couple. I'd stuck my head in the mud with her for a little while and showed her that I cared for her, but she was clearly upset about something.

A: I was trying to figure out how to bring up what was bothering me without making Chad feel like I was attacking him or making him feel like a jerk while I was processing all my feelings.

I felt the Holy Spirit was gently saying to me, "You *could* avoid bringing it up to Chad, but this is a chance to grow closer to him and to understand each other more deeply."

I wanted an open, honest relationship. The Holy Spirit never seemed to tire of challenging me by asking, Do you *really* want that kind of openness, or are you just going to hold on to what you're feeling and settle for faux comfort?

I didn't like that question. I'd learned that though faux comfort initially feels real, it eventually comes back to sabotage you. Sure, I could spare myself the temporary tension of talking about how I felt with zero guarantee of the response. But that would leave me with the internal turmoil of not sharing what I was feeling, which would likely lead to me distancing myself from Chad.

I needed more time to process. But then Chad asked me . . .

C: "Is something bothering you?"

A: *Crap, I need more time.*
Where's my script?
Oh, hey there, stress.
Nice of you to join.
[Awkward silence.]
Well, here we are. Might as well rip off the Band-Aid.
"Are you uncomfortable talking about my reality as a Black woman?"

C: "No, babe, what makes you ask that?" I could sense Adaeze's discomfort, and it caught me off guard. Adaeze is typically very confident and well spoken, especially in the midst of any sort of conflict.

A: "Because it seems like you keep skirting around how my experience at that table was different from yours."

C: "I wasn't trying to skirt around your experience. I realize those looks made you uncomfortable, but it was just people looking."

A: "Okay." *Do I even wanna try to explain this?*

C: I was starting to feel a little defensive. I mean, yeah, I saw people looking, but it wasn't a blatant attack on us. Frankly, I didn't understand why we were stuck on this topic. "I get that you see we are different, but I'm proud of what you are and what makes you different. It sucks that the world is the way it is." *Now that was good.*

A: *Wait. Did he just "what" me?* "What do you mean, you're proud of *what* I am?"

C: I needed to reassure Adaeze that I understood that our life experiences were different. So, once again, I pointed at her headwrap and doubled down on what I honestly thought was the statement of the night.

"I will still kiss you and hold your hand even when you are wearing that!"

A: It *was* the statement of the night. Just not the way he thought it was. The narrative I heard was that Chad saw me only in the ways I was different from him: all my metaphorical headwraps. In other words, all the ways people viewed the two of us negatively fell on me.

When he repeated the statement, it felt like a betrayal of safety—like a confirmation of the pain I was already feeling. Worse, it solidified to me that Chad didn't really understand what I was talking about. It was the first time it had dawned on me that our relationship might not work. I loved being with Chad, but I didn't want him to be with me *in spite of* me.

It was all unraveling.

Do I have the energy to do this with him, or is he just never going to get it?

Maybe Chad's not ready for this.

Maybe I'm not ready for this.

Maybe this is too dangerous for my heart.

In the past, I had spoken up and whistle-blown in white circles an exhausting number of times—to what felt like no avail. Now it seemed like history was repeating itself. So, in order to protect myself, I subconsciously started to check out.

When we got back to Chad's place, I just wanted to get away, be alone, process. I didn't want to make any rash decisions. I wanted to leave, but I really needed to pee. So as soon as we got inside, as nonchalantly as possible, I told Chad I needed to use his bathroom.

C: I wouldn't exactly describe Adaeze as nonchalant at that moment.

A: I locked myself in the bathroom and took a moment to look at myself in the mirror—taking in my headwrap, taking in *me*. I tried to reaffirm myself with an internal pep talk.

Everything you are is worth loving and appreciating.

But I felt like I couldn't win either way. If I tried to explain what I was feeling, Chad would likely hear that he's an awful person—even though I knew he wasn't intentionally trying to hurt me. But if I *didn't* say anything, I'd feel even more isolated, and nothing would get resolved.

I'd been in an interracial relationship years before that had failed miserably. After that ex got enough pressure from his family, he decided I wasn't worth the trouble. Even after I'd genuinely tried to explain my side of things, it wasn't enough. Or rather, *I* wasn't enough. At least that was the false truth I had to unlearn from that painful situation. And now here I was again. Woulda been nice if I could have googled some kind of manual on how to explain things like a perfect Black person, but that would be too easy.

With tears welling in my eyes, I reached up and slowly undid my headwrap, thinking, *I don't know if I can be my full self here, so I need to go.* I wasn't breaking it off with Chad. I just felt like I needed to get out of there and at least take a break from thinking about it for the night.

I looked away from my reflection, as if leaving that inner conversation. *Not now. Wait till you get home to process all this.*

After I finished in the bathroom, I took a deep breath in an attempt to still my emotions and headed back downstairs. *Maybe I can sneak out of the house . . .*

C: Meanwhile, blissfully unaware that Adaeze was questioning our entire relationship, I was getting out the blankets and trying to make the living room look slightly less like the grayscale bachelor pad it was so we could watch a movie.

When she came downstairs, I noticed it immediately. *She took off the headwrap.*

Even worse, she did not come over to the couch, where I was sitting. Instead, she walked over to the table, where she'd put her purse, keys, and phone. *Maybe she just wants to be more comfortable. Maybe she just wants her phone.*

Then she went for her jacket. This was the moment the anvil finally fell on Wile E. Coyote's head. Something was horrendously wrong here. I just had no idea what it was.

A: "I think I'm going to go home."

C: She turned to leave, so I moved between her and the door. I had already learned that when Adaeze is upset, she tends to physically and/or emotionally run away. I wouldn't try to stop her from leaving if she wanted to go—I just wanted her to stay long enough to have a conversation. The look on her face made it clear: my ignorance had hurt her more than anyone in the brewery had.

Not wanting her to feel trapped, I asked, "Could we please go for a walk?"

A: Chad's humble request to go for a walk crumbled some of my walls. I didn't take off my headwrap to wake him up, but the fact that it made him realize that maybe he didn't get it was somewhat of a relief. Not to say that his—dare I say—*ignorance* didn't hurt, because it definitely did. A lot. But the fact that he was so desperately trying to get me to stay and talk so he could understand what I was feeling was encouraging.

Even though everything in me was screaming, *This will be hard and maybe suck*, something told me he was worth fighting for.

So I said, "Okay." After being burned multiple times in the past, I considered that real growth.

As we stepped out into the cool of the evening, Chad put his arm around me. I was as stiff as a stick, with my arms crossed. We walked in silence for a while. Then Chad spoke.

C: "I'm sorry. Apparently, I *really* don't understand what's going on. Could you help me understand?"

A: *Let's see if the third time's the charm.* "Can you explain more what you meant by the headwrap thing?"

C: "Of course! All I wanted to do was let you know that I am here for you and want to be there with you during moments like that in the brewery. I see that the world is different for you than it is for me. Your headwrap was something that embodies your culture and makes you who you are, so I was using that as an example. When we go out and you are proudly showing off your Black culture, I will be there with you and be proud of you. People can look all they want and think whatever they want about you, but I still want to be the person with you. It doesn't matter if they think you are wrong, because you are being who you are. I think you're beautiful. Even if you do something that makes me uncomfortable, I will still be there."

I went on for another fifteen minutes or so, and Adaeze, being the gracious human she is, patiently listened to my rant—silently, with her arms crossed.

Finally, I gave up. "Why don't you tell me what upset you?"

A: I took a beat. I was mentally calculating how to say this right and be the perfect Black person. You know, the Black person who has the perfect way of talking about tough race stuff so the white listener won't incorrectly think I'm saying they're racist. The Black person who can oh-so-effortlessly call out micro-aggressions and educate in a way that leaves the white listener inspired, changed, and empowered, all at once.

For the record, it really meant a lot that he tried, but listening to him explain his headwrap comment yet again only reinforced what had hurt me in the first place.

"I know you weren't trying to be hurtful when you said that comment about the headwrap, but it hurt me. I don't want to be seen as the person whose differences you have to put up with. I don't wanna be the person you nobly fall on your sword to show up with, as if you are a martyr doing me a favor—as if you're the hero who is valiantly and humbly *still* showing up with me, *even though* I am wearing a headwrap."

I took a steadying deep breath and continued, "When you

say, 'I'll show up or be seen with you even if you are wearing that,' the story that tells me is that when I wear a headwrap to express who I am and rep my culture, you have to look past it in order to be a good boyfriend. That makes it seem like I can't fully be me if I want you to be fully comfortable. And I can't do that. I hear your heart in what you are trying to say, but what you are communicating doesn't feel good. It's distancing and makes me feel less than. It separates me from *us* and makes me the different one, the problem. It makes me feel like I am so different, and you are normal. And I get that to you, you're normal, and I'm different. But I don't want to feel like you are doing me a solid by being with me or like you're taking one for the team by still showing up with me if I'm wearing whatever I want to wear. It makes it seem like you're with me *in spite of me*. I want you to be with me for *me*. I want us to be on the same playing field, in this together. You have now made that comment repeatedly, which reinforces that this is how you feel. If that's the case, I'm not even gonna ask you to change. I'm just telling you why it hurts and why it's making me question *us*."

C: The more I listened, the more my eyes started to open. Without even realizing it, I had drawn a delineation between myself and Adaeze because of her skin color. It was not my intention, but she was right. I had a white savior complex at the restaurant. I *was* trying to nobly fall on my sword for her. And without meaning to, I had made Adaeze feel less than, instead of feeling like the beautiful gift of God she is. Not only had I failed miserably in our first deep dive into racial conversations, but I had hurt her deeply.

I was starting to realize that as close as Adaeze and I were, there was still a deep well of conversations we needed to have. We had only just scratched the surface.

CHAPTER 1

AS DIFFERENT AS BLACK AND WHITE

C: Sometimes, white people, we just suck, and I hate that. I hate it for my wife, for my friends, and for all people of color. The truth is, too often, we knowingly or unknowingly say and do things that, at best, marginalize and, at worst, hurt people of color deeply. It's not always intentional. It's just a reality of the cultural beast we have created.

The thing I—as a white man—had to learn right off the bat is that, in Western culture, white is seen as "normal." Everything else is "different." It's that simple. Adaeze has been saturated in white culture her entire life without having to seek it out, and yet her normal and my normal look very, very different—and they have from the very beginning.

WHERE WE COME FROM

A: My Jesus-loving, intentional parents were born and raised in Nigeria. After they were married, they moved to London to pursue their medical licenses, which is where my three awesome, perfect-balance-of-protective older brothers and I were born. When I was two, we moved to Tulsa, Oklahoma—the heart of the Bible Belt—because my parents wanted to send us to Christian schools, and the schools in London were not up to their spiritual standards.

My parents never really taught us about differences in people, and it seemed like they never had to. They just led by example. They instilled in us a confidence in Jesus Christ and a sense of pride as Nigerian Americans.

They were the first in their families to leave Nigeria. Once our relatives saw that we had all survived, a lot of them followed our family to the States, and it didn't take long for my brothers and me to figure out that we did not live up to their expectations. For example, our aunts and uncles would expectantly speak Igbo to us, only to have us stare blankly back or mispronounce one of the few words we did know, resulting in a disdainful "Chai!" or some other *tsk-tsk* of disapproval. Though our parents never forced us to fit our relatives' expectations, I was still very aware that, in my extended family's eyes, I wasn't Nigerian enough.

Ironically, people in Tulsa always made sure to point out that my parents still had their Nigerian "accent," to which my mom would semijokingly retort, "I don't have an accent; *you* have an accent!" She wasn't wrong. Where she was from, everyone talked like her. Still, she never understood why everyone kept pointing it out. Frankly, neither did I.

I learned the word *accent* from Tulsans who labeled my parents' voices that way. And whenever the word was uttered, it dripped with so much "otherness" that I could understand why my mom developed a disdain for the word.

C: Obviously, my parents are not Nigerian, and I definitely was not born in London. I was born in Pennsylvania, but we moved to Spokane, Washington, when I was in second grade. Both my parents spent their childhoods in Virginia, and they carried those Southern manners with them all the way out to the Pacific Northwest. My mom, for example, would bring home-baked cookies to the new neighbors when they moved in (which apparently wasn't a thing in the PNW). And as a proper Southern lady, she was always appalled to see people walking around the grocery stores in sweatpants.

And, yes, people made comments on my parents' Southern accents and habits when I was growing up. However, most of the comments were endearing. They would usually come in the form of something like, "Oh, your mom is just so cute!" or "I just love your parents—they are so nice!" Southern hospitality really shines when not everybody does it.

I never felt like I was all that different from the people around me. I acted like my friends. I dressed like my friends. I looked like my friends. Even though my family was Southern, I always identified as being from the upper-left USA. It was all I knew, and I seemed to fit in there.

A: Being the only Black girl in my class—or one of three Black kids, at most—I experienced "otherness" early and often.

Since my maiden name is Azubuike, 99.9 percent of the time I was the first name on a teacher's roll call list. And 99.9 percent of the time, the teacher's eyes would widen in fear as she stared at the first entry on the list that had both a first name *and* a last name she was terrified to attempt.

I had to decide if I was gonna let them stumble through it, *juuuust* to see if they might get it right, or if I should help them out and try to hide my exasperation at once again having to provide the correct pronunciation of my perfectly-normal-sounding-to-me name.

Thankfully, my name wasn't an object of ridicule at school. My hair, on the other hand . . .

One day, when I was in middle school, a strong gust of wind tore through the playground and took my not-so-clipped-in clip-in extension piece with it. All the kids laughed.

Somehow, I wasn't seriously embarrassed. I retrieved my hairpiece, briefly chased a boy who was laughing the loudest, reattached it to my head, and wore it the rest of the day. I don't think I even told anyone in my family about the incident when I got home. But it's making its way into this book, so clearly it had *some* effect on me.

Then, when I was in ninth grade, we were coming back from a field trip, and a loudmouth was throwing paper airplanes on the bus. One of the planes landed in my box braids. The boy laughed, pointed, and yelled out in a voice far too loud for even a bus, "Haha! The plane got caught in your Jheri curl!"

His comment struck me as wrong in so many ways. For one thing, Jheri curl wasn't even remotely close to the hairstyle I was rocking. Think the hairstyle of Michael Jackson versus nineties Brandy. What I couldn't have put into words back then but now know is that it was racist enough for this white boy to make fun of my hair in any way. But for him to ignorantly toss out an incorrect Black hairstyle in the process was even more degrading. Besides, his joke didn't even land. There were a few uncomfortable courtesy laughs, and I removed the plane from my hair and tossed it on the ground, unamused.

My full lips were also a source of fascination for people. It's not that the comments were always bad, but it always struck me as interesting that nobody commented on the not-so-full lips of the white girls in class. I mean, what an odd topic of discussion among children, no?

C: In stark contrast to Adaeze, I was privileged in almost every way in school. I was never bullied, I felt totally secure, and I never felt alone or singled out in my community. By the time I was in high school, I was spending every waking moment playing any sport I could.

A: Playing sports was a wonderful outlet for me as well, especially in AAU (Amateur Athletic Union) basketball. Because we played outside our own school district, there was a lot more diversity in AAU ball, which opened my world and made me feel less alone, less "only," and less "different."

I also went on a lot of school-sponsored mission trips to places like Juárez, Reynosa, and Nuevo Laredo, Mexico, which exposed me to some of the world outside our little Tulsa bubble and my Nigerian-American home.

C: Diversity wasn't even a discussion for me growing up. My school was so white that we got away with joking about having two and a half Black kids at our school. (Five of my classmates had interracial parents.)

Then, when I was in high school, there was a bomb threat. It was a mess. We went into lockdown, the buses had to come late, and all after-school programs were canceled that day. We even made the local news.

Believe it or not, the bomb threat ended up not being the main story from the day. As it happened, the reporter who came out to cover the incident was a Black woman, and while she was filming the story, a kid from my school drove his truck, with Confederate flag in tow, right behind her and yelled a racial slur out his window. Our school was definitely on the news that day, but the bomb threat became the setting for the story about harassment of the reporter.

Even though I was sheltered from my own biases at the time, I remember being so disappointed that this would happen at my high school.

Another time, at a volleyball game, a friend of mine pulled out his flip phone, and I noticed he had changed his background to a Confederate flag.

I lost it. I said, "What are you, some kind of redneck?"

A: Wait a minute. Isn't redneck *also* technically a slur?

C: Yeah . . . probably not my finest moment. But at least I said something.

Looking back, I am sure there were other racially charged situations happening around me, but I honestly wasn't aware of them. (I'm not proud of that either.) All that to say, I grew up in a community that tended to wear blinders when it came to issues of race.

A: Conversely, a lot of racially tense situations were happening around me, and I was *very* much aware of them.

In college, one of my closest white male friends told me I was "the whitest Black girl" he knew. I didn't even know what to do with that, but I knew I didn't like it.

When I got a job as a full-time worship leader at a predominantly white megachurch, I was told that one of the worship staff members thought I was "too much" on stage.

One day, I was standing at the door of the sanctuary after a worship service, my hair in a French warrior braid to the side. As people were filing out, a white grown man told me, "Your hair looks like a snake!"

A long-time white female congregant told me, "You know, it's so *interesting* having someone different like you on stage." And yet, when a white male friend mentioned he'd been to my church and had heard me sing, he commented, "You sound white."

I was told by fellow worship staff members that the songs I wrote or wanted to sing during church services were "too gospel" and that some of the songs I wanted to put in the pre- and post-service music that played over the speakers weren't our church's style. (The irony is, after I left, that same church jumped on the "gospel is cool!" bandwagon that erupted during the racial reconciliation movement and started doing songs with big-name Black female artists.)

Whether it was the way I talked, sang, led worship, wrote songs, or dressed, whether it was my volume level or my "extraness," a common theme among white people around me was to define my Blackness by their own standards of what was "Black enough" or "too Black" for them.

Whether I was at school or at work/church, every space I showed up in resulted in me having to prove I belonged, underscoring the narrative that all the things that made me "different" were either bad or wrong.

Subconsciously, I began building walls around myself to survive.

IF YOU'RE "NORMAL," THAT WOULD MAKE ME...

C: Having spent the first twenty years of my life in a white bubble, I didn't know anything outside my own world. My parents and

WHITE BOY / BLACK GIRL

grandparents had grown up in segregated churches and cultures that believed interracial relationships were a sin.

Even as a kid, I saw, to some extent, how this diminished the fullness of Black people's humanity. My family was firmly planted in a culture that was harshly divided between "us" and "them." Even worse, they had been taught for generations that this was totally acceptable. We were "normal." People of color were "different."

A: Living in a culture that's not only predominantly white but "white normalized" means that the predominant view of the world is filtered through a white lens. When the white experience becomes centralized like this, it's easy to look at everything else as wrong, less than, or strange. This, in turn, creates division—especially when we're not aware of it.

Statements like "You're so [well-spoken/pretty/educated/fill-in-the-blank] for a Black person" come directly from a place of white normalization. The white experience ends up being placed unapologetically on the person of color, in addition to everything else they are already carrying.

C: This is part of the reason the headwrap incident was so hurtful to Adaeze. When I said, "I will still kiss you and hold your hand even when you are wearing that!" what she heard was "I am okay with how different you are." What I *should* have said was "Adaeze, I am just excited to be here with you. Our differences are a gift, and it's a shame other people don't see it that way." In other words, I should have simply appreciated her for the wonderful creation of God she is, as opposed to making her feel singled out for expressing herself in a way that is every bit as normal to her as my Vans and flannel hoodie were to me.

I think this is where white people go wrong most of the time. White normalization renders us insensitive to the reality of people of color. I don't have to think about being a white man. On the other hand, Adaeze is reminded every day of her life that she is a Black woman.

In fact, as we are having this conversation, we are sitting in a coffee shop surrounded by white people. Adaeze just felt the need to pause midthought to tell me that she is very aware of that and she's worried about how they might feel if they heard what we're talking about. While I fully expect that some white people would be offended by our discussion, it never once occurred to me that I should speak more quietly or pause to let someone pass our table before continuing. Adaeze, on the other hand, has to be on automatic, almost constant, alert not to say or do anything that might ruffle someone's feathers.

WHITE MEN WALKING

C: A few months after we started dating, we took a trip to North Carolina for Adaeze's birthday. One of Adaeze's best friends was living in Charlotte, and some of my best friends live in Asheville and Durham, so we thought this would be a great chance to introduce each other to important friends of ours, as well as have some time away together.

We were with two of my friends, driving along the winding roads of the Blue Ridge Mountains in the backcountry of North Carolina one morning, when it hit us: we were stupid hungry. Luckily, my friends knew of a diner close by. When we pulled in, there were a couple of big trucks in the parking lot—and I mean *big* pickups, not the little Tesla sedans we're used to seeing around Denver. We definitely weren't in the city anymore.

A few people stared at us as we got out of the car, but I didn't think much of it.

When we walked in, it felt like we had taken a time machine back to the 1960s. All the booths in the dining area were upholstered in sparkly red leather, with white Formica tables between the seats. Red rope lights ran along the floor and the top of the walls, almost like crown molding. The only nod to the "modern" era was the jukebox, which had been placed front and center and played cassette tapes instead of vinyl records.

The second we stepped through the doors, every eye locked on us, freezing us in place.

A: They weren't the kind of stares where you wondered if maybe they were looking at a clock directly behind your head. These stares felt dangerous. If looks could talk, these would clearly be saying, "We don't approve of you, Black woman. And we don't approve of you being with her, white man."

It was bad.

Chad's arm immediately swung around my shoulder and didn't drop the whole time we were there. I was trying to be strong, but I didn't dare make eye contact with anyone. As we followed the hostess to our table, the stares followed us, bodies slowly turning, every eye zeroing in on me.

I *really* didn't want to eat there. But it didn't seem like Chad's friends were even aware of the way everyone was staring at me, and I didn't want to ruin everybody else's good time.

C: Not to pile on (doing it anyway), but the food wasn't even that good. No doubt, we could have gotten the same quality at the gas station next door. I was very aware that Adaeze felt uncomfortable. But instead of suggesting that we leave, I just held on to her tighter. I wanted to show her that she wasn't alone, that she was safe with me.

A: However, even with Chad's arm around me, I still felt alone and unsafe. Worse, I felt like I was on display—as if I was being seen but for all the wrong reasons.

And yet we stayed.

It was one of the most uncomfortable breakfasts of my life.

The next morning, we were getting ready to leave Chad's friends' house, and I was sitting by myself in the living room, which had huge floor-to-ceiling windows. I was just about to take my bags out to the car when two white men walked past the house wearing camo pants. One was wearing a matching camo T-shirt, and the other was wearing a T-shirt with a Confederate flag covering the front and back.

Now I will own that I 100 percent profiled them based on the experience I'd had at the diner the previous day. Still, they were walking with such purpose that, to me, it almost felt as though they were out hunting Black people or something.

Even though I was well aware they had no idea I was there, I no longer felt safe taking my bags out to the car alone. Instead, I stayed where I was, watching the men until they disappeared into a garage at the end of the road.

Then Chad came into the room.

C: Actually, I had been there the entire time.

A: Are you sure? I could have sworn I was alone.

C: And *that* is the point we're trying to make. Just like at the diner, even though I was physically there, emotionally, Adaeze still felt alone.

A: Chad's friends walked into the room, and one of them asked, "What are you guys looking at?"

   I froze.

   "There were . . . some guys . . . walking," I started. "And, uh . . . one was, um, wearing all camo . . . and the other was wearing Confederate flags . . ." I quietly trailed off.

   I didn't want to offend them. After all, these were two of Chad's closest friends, and I wanted to make a good impression. Plus, this was where they lived. What if they knew those guys?

C: I could feel Adaeze's hesitation, so I jumped in. "There was a guy walking outside with a Confederate flag on his shirt. It was pretty uncomfortable." How I thought that made things clearer, I have no idea.

A: You tried, babe.

   And he had. But all that did was trigger past experiences when I've tried to explain something about race to white people. It doesn't land, and then a white person valiantly says, "I think what Adaeze is trying to say is . . ." They proceed to repeat literally the exact same thing I just said, and all the white people in the room suddenly get it.

   As if on cue, his other friend immediately chimed in with "Well, that's just how the world is," which to me translated to "Well, that sucks, but that's your problem" or "Guess you just have to deal with it."

C: In my friends' defense, they weren't trying to be rude or hurtful. They're both genuinely sweet people. It was just a classic normalized statement coming from a place of white privilege.

Unintentional as the comment was, on the heels of what had already unfolded that weekend, it served as yet another wedge separating "us" from "them"—as if Adaeze needed to feel any more "other" there, of all places, in a very rural, very white, very backwoods mountain town.

STEP OUT AND STEP UP

C: Ultimately, what happened in North Carolina isn't all that different from experiences we've had in other parts of the country. Even now, I have to consciously remind myself that, more often than not, Adaeze is dealing with a completely different reality than I am.

This is a very apples-to-oranges example, but my first job out of grad school was at a physical therapy clinic where I was the only guy among six female coworkers. I got along well with everybody, but after about a year, I realized that I could not talk about that Sunday's football game with anyone around me. The women were much less entertained by the guy at the gym who looked like a fool using the squat rack to do some curls, and whenever I wanted to go grab a beer after work, my coworkers all wanted to get martinis or some fruity white wine. If I wanted to be included, it felt like my only option was to go along with what the women wanted to do, because they were the majority.

Granted, this doesn't even come close to what Adaeze has had to deal with. My point is simply that when you are in the minority, what you want, like, feel, or need often takes a back seat to what the majority wants, likes, feels, or needs. And after a while, it can feel very isolating.

A: To our white friends in any kind of interracial relationship—romantic or otherwise—I have a loving challenge for you: the next time you are with that person and you have an opportunity to do so, step out of your position of privilege for a moment and allow yourself to be uncomfortable along with them. Look at the room through their eyes. Especially if you know this has been a thing for your loved one in the past, take notice of how many people of color are (or are not) in the room. Consider the conversation that is taking place from their perspective. Make a mental note of who the waitstaff addresses at your table, the tone used when your friend is being spoken to, and the way others look at them. Think about what they're having to work around that you aren't.

I know—this isn't comfortable. And it might take a little practice. But the more aware you are of your counterpart's different-from-yours reality, the more keen you will be to do something about it. Hopefully, the more you empathize with the challenges faced by those you are in relationship with, the more empowered you will feel to speak up for friends and colleagues, especially if their voice isn't as respected a voice as yours. You can then hold others accountable for missteps, accidental or otherwise. Because, let's be honest, most people take it better when they're put in their place by someone who looks like them.

For example, if Chad had stepped out of the privilege of being considered "normal" at the diner, instead of simply noticing that I was uncomfortable and lovingly putting his arm around me, he might have taken a moment to think about how he would feel if the looks coming my way were directed at him. He might have taken his response a step further by asking his friends if we could go somewhere else.

Once the situation was brought to light for his friends, they might have been willing to step out of their normal and oblige that request—even if they didn't understand why—and then ask follow-up questions to better understand why the situation was upsetting to me.

As for the reaction to the guys wearing camo and Confederate flags, Chad's friend could have stepped out of his privilege by offering a more sincere statement, such as "I hate that this is the way the world is sometimes." It doesn't solve the problem, but at least it shows an attempt to empathize and sit with me in it.

Basically, it's a matter of stepping into the other person's shoes and asking yourself, *How would I want to be treated right now?* As the Bible says, "In everything, do to others what you would have them do to you, for this sums up the Law and the Prophets" (Matthew 7:12).

C: Amen to that.

Right about now, if you're white, you may be thinking, *Wait . . . why is it on me to do this? Why should I be the only one to inconvenience myself?*

The reality is that our friends of color have already been asked to deal with more than anybody has the right to ask. If we aren't willing to sacrifice our own comfort (and not in a martyr-type way, where we're constantly reminding the person of color that we're doing them a favor), that relationship will always be at a disadvantage. Not because of the person of color—because of us.

We are the ones who created the playing field we're on (whether we realize it or not), and we have essentially said to our friends of color, "If you want to play here, you need to fit into our box." If we want to start erasing racial boundaries, it stands to reason that the people who created the boundary should cross first. Taking the first step is like extending an olive branch and saying, "If you are willing to trust me, I am willing to learn."

We need to be willing! It is easy to love when someone walks, talks, acts, and looks like us. But if we really care about someone, then their feelings, their safety, and their comfort should matter just as much, if not more, than our own. It's like Paul says in his letter to the Corinthians: "Love . . . does not dishonor others, it is not self-seeking" (1 Corinthians 13:4-5).

C & A: If we want to level the playing field, we need to honor and seek the best for each other. Look at all the times in the New Testament when Jesus invited someone considered "different" by society into His circle—often at the expense of His own optics.

Jesus asked the Samaritan woman for water at the well (John 4). Jews at the time would not talk to Samaritans, let alone one with a questionable relationship status, yet Jesus approached her. And that isn't even mentioning the male/female dynamic, which was considered taboo in that context. He was breaking all the rules for the sake of inclusion.

Jesus ate at the tax collector's table, which was also frowned upon (Luke chapters 5 and 19). Tax collectors were viewed as traitors by the Jews because they were ethnically Jewish but collected money from their own people on behalf of the Romans. Going into the home of a tax collector and sitting down for a meal would have been seen as cozying up with the enemy.

Then there was the time Jesus healed the man with leprosy (Matthew 8). There was so much fear and stigma attached to leprosy in Jesus' day that they were forced to live outside the city. Yet Jesus laid His hands on the man—an act that would have been unthinkable to most Jews in His day.

Likewise, Jesus healed a man who was blind and was considered an outcast (John 9). People believed this man's blindness was the result of sin, but Jesus treated him with dignity.

Time and time again, Jesus took the first step, reaching out to the disenfranchised and putting the needs of others before His own.

What about us? We all have people in our lives who could benefit from a little selflessness and grace on our part. Are we willing to get uncomfortable to show them love?

A: I think I speak for a lot of people of color when I say that we don't want our white friends to feel like we're waiting for them to attend to us. We just want them to be aware that the realities we live in are often vastly different.

Knowing that Chad is aware of these dueling realities—and that we're on the same team—gives me the freedom to vent to him without fearing he will make me feel guilty for not being "strong enough" when it hurts. It also gives Chad the freedom to learn from my experiences without feeling guilty for not always recognizing microaggressions when they happen.

We're not only aware of white privilege and normalization— we're in it *together*.

Also, my fellow people of color, you all best believe I'm preaching to myself on this next one because this is something I'm constantly working on: we need to be better at being unoffendable. That doesn't mean we don't feel pain when people act ignorantly or discriminate against us. It just means we need to work at protecting ourselves from being offended while also educating others for the sake of improving our relationships.

We can do the work of realizing that cultural ignorance (e.g., Chad not realizing the impact of his comment about my headwrap or his friends not understanding why two white men wearing camo gear and Confederate flags might make me uncomfortable) is not the same as intentional offenses (e.g., the way the locals stared me down in the diner or the guy at Chad's high school shouted a racial slur at the reporter). If we do, it will help us have grace for ourselves when we do get offended, as well as for the person who acted not out of malice but out of ignorance.

When we don't make that effort, we end up with shorter fuses, we're more likely to walk away or shut down a conversation (like I almost did with Chad after the headwrap incident), and we're more prone to build walls to protect ourselves—and, in the process, lock the other person out.

The goal of every interracial relationship—and of this book—should be to tear down those walls, to learn to communicate honestly and effectively, and to move forward together. We can't do that if one party isn't willing to take the first step into the other's reality or if we won't let them in when they do.

This is where the redemptive work of Jesus is paramount. When we surrender our prejudice and pain at the feet of Jesus, He will heal us and help us learn, and we will treat each other better as a result.

Case in point: I remember being at Target one time waiting for a self-checkout kiosk to open up, and I overheard a conversation between the white mom in line behind me and her young blond-haired daughter.

"Mommy, look at her dark skin!" the daughter said, loud enough for everyone in the self-checkout area to hear.

My defenses immediately went up as I waited to see how the

mom would react, fully expecting to hear the usual embarrassed and uncomfortable, "Shhh . . . we don't say that," which would have communicated to the little girl that my chocolate skin was somehow bad or less-than.

But to my surprise, the mom didn't shush the girl, nor did she attach a shameful or negative connotation to what her daughter had just said. Instead, my heart warmed when the mother simply replied, "Yeah, sweetie, isn't she pretty?"

To which the little girl replied in drawn-out wonder, "Yeah!"

I wanted to turn around and personally thank that mom, but I thought it might be a bit too much. Instead, I just let her continue to be the boss mom that she is. Maybe someday she'll read this book and remember that day. Either way, I hope she knows what a positive effect her response had—not only on her daughter but on me and everyone else listening.

C: As awesome as that one mother was, the reality is true racial reconciliation is not something we have the power to tackle alone. We need Jesus to come back and restore the world to its original design, fully restored to the Father, and fully healed as it will be in the end.

C & A: Whether you are a Christian or not, the reality is, if we want our interracial relationships to improve, we need a lot of help navigating these often awkward and uncomfortable situations and conversations.

Speaking of which . . .

CHAPTER 2

LET THE AWKWARD CONVERSATIONS BEGIN!

C: I remember the first conversation Adaeze and I ever had about race.

I had been volunteering as a guitar player for the worship team Adaeze was leading, and we'd been friends for about a year and a half.

It's not that I didn't find Adaeze attractive. In fact, I thought she was smokin' hot. But I didn't dare ask her out because she was on staff at the church, and as one of seven guitar players— and a volunteer—I was expendable. So, odds were, if anything went wrong, I'd have been out the door.

Granted, that didn't stop me from strategically positioning myself onstage in a place that would allow the Lord to show me His glory through the view that is Adaeze from behind. (Keeping it PG-13 for the Lord here.)

A: Full disclosure: I thought Chad was a good-lookin' man. But because of the leader-volunteer dynamic, we kept things very platonic. Until . . .

C: Our church opened a new location, and I felt the Lord calling me to join the launch team. After our last service together, I asked Adaeze to go get tacos and a beer with me so I could let her know that I was going to leave her worship team to help at the new campus. This became our accidental first date.

A: After we got to the restaurant, we started talking about dating within the church—not each other, just in general. I told Chad that another white guy friend of mine had recently told me, "Most white guys in Colorado will not find you attractive because they didn't grow up with Black women. So even though they might see you and think, *She's pretty*, they probably won't be attracted to you."

C: Then she flat out asked me . . .

A: "Have you ever found a Black woman attractive?"

C: "Of course."

A: "Like who?"

C: I knew I couldn't say Beyoncé, you know . . . the *one* Black girl every white guy knows. I had to have an intelligent answer, so I said, "Gabrielle Union." At that point, Adaeze looked at me with a twinkle in her eye, did a little hair flip, and said . . .

A: "So, for research purposes only . . . do you find *me* attractive?"

My brothers often told me, "Adaeze, guys are hunters, but don't be afraid to break a few sticks." I thought I was being subtle in tryna drop a hint. You know, just casually snapping some sticks like Bambi, tiptoeing through the forest . . .

C: When, in actuality, she was barreling through the woods, chopping down trees like Paul freaking Bunyan!

Without hesitation, I told her, "Yeah."

A: I promptly sat up straighter in my seat, pleasantly surprised at the sexy confidence with which he so quickly responded.

In light of our new revelation, I asked, "What would happen if you brought a Black girl home with you?"

C: Here's where things got interesting. Adaeze and I had reached the point where we felt pretty comfortable around each other, so I just gave it to her straight. "Well, my grandparents are from Virginia. They live on a farm a couple miles from the farms they were both born on, and . . . they believe that interracial marriage is a sin."

A: *Crap,* I thought. *Here we go again.*

I had been down this road before, and it hadn't ended well. The question was . . . was Chad worth going down that road again?

C: The next day, I called my parents and said, "I think I went on a date with Adaeze."

They knew who she was from worship videos I'd shown

them, and I'd mentioned her name several times. I expected them to be excited—or at the very least happy that I was finally dating *anyone*—and to say something like "Oh, Chad, that's great! Tell us more about her!"

What I got was, "Do you have any idea what you're getting into? What your *kids* would have to deal with?"

I was floored. We had gone on one date. Why were we talking about kids?

They kept going. "Have you thought about what your life will look like five, ten years down the road? What are we supposed to tell your grandparents?"

In fairness, I knew this would throw them for a loop. Like most parents, my mom and dad had a picture in their minds of how my life would turn out, and me being with a Black woman was definitely not in that picture. It never even occurred to them that I would bring home a girl who was anything other than white. Needless to say, this was just the first of many conversations we would have on the subject.

Two weeks of said conversations later, Adaeze hit me with . . .

A: "I think you should take the next twenty-four hours to really think about whether you're ready for this."

We'd been spending more time together, but we hadn't yet made things official between us. Before my heart got further into this, I wanted to give Chad some space to consider how many more of these conversations he was willing to have just to be with me.

C: I didn't need twenty-four hours. I'd been wrestling with that question ever since my parents asked me if I had any idea what

I was getting myself into. That said, *was* I actually ready for an interracial relationship?

Was I ready to go against everything my family expected of me?

Was I ready for my grandparents to potentially disown me?

Was I ready for all the tension, hurt feelings, and disappointment?

Was I ready for the endless arguments?

In my mind, it all came down to one thing: Did I believe in my heart that Adaeze was 100 percent worth it?

Yes. I did. So, yes, I was ready—even if my family wasn't.

A: My family, on the other hand, already had two beautiful interracial marriages in it. Growing up in a predominantly white city, my parents never seemed to care who we ended up with as long as they loved Jesus and were on fire for God. Chad checked both boxes.

After I told my family about our date, one of my brothers joked, "We already have two white people married into the family. I was hoping maybe you'd end up with a Black man." And while he eventually apologized to both of us for saying that, I considered myself blessed that this was the worst thing anyone in my family had to say about our relationship.

C: Some members of my family, on the other hand, had plenty to say. As Adaeze and I continued to see each other, things got tense quickly—not between Adaeze and me, but from all the voices coming at us in the form of letters, phone calls, Facetime calls, and personal interactions.

I mean, it got bad. During those first two months, we got hit with . . .

"You need to make sure she's not trying to get something from you."

"You need to think about what your children will look like."

"I still dream of you finding a sweet little Southern girl."

"If you make your bed hard, you'll have to sleep in it."

"You'll never be allowed in churches again."

"Your relationship is hurting *my* relationship with people I care about."

"You need to choose someone who will be accepted in the real world."

And possibly the most ludicrous: "You could be beheaded for this!"

C & A: Hang on a sec while we cry it out together.

Honestly, looking back, it's almost hard to believe we even made it through those first two months.

The truth is, we almost didn't.

We often say that we weren't afforded the luxury of a honeymoon phase. You know, where you both pretend you're perfect, and for some reason, the other person actually believes it. We had to get real with each other really quickly because we had to deal with so many outside forces trying to drive a wedge between us, and there was simply no time to fake it.

In fact, we were almost a year and a half into our relationship before we had our first real fight. Even then, after everything we had gone through early on, the typical relationship stuff felt easy in comparison.

C: It helped that Adaeze and I agreed that any time my family said things like this to me, we would talk about it. I knew their comments would hurt her even more than they hurt me, and some were more difficult to talk about than others. She wanted to know, though, so I told her even when I had reservations.

That decision—to share whatever came at us, like we did with the headwrap situation—set the foundation for our relationship on talking honestly and learning from each other.

The worst of it came in the form of a letter I received a couple of months into dating from someone particularly close to me. I won't go into details since we have now reconciled, but suffice it to say that the comments were extremely hurtful.

A: I read that letter over and over again, trying to make sense of the words scribbled on the page by Chad's loved one. I tried to give the person the benefit of the doubt, despite the hurtful nature of what they'd written.

However, as I sat there crying, all I could think was, *It's happening again.*

I had been the Black wedge in a white family before. When it happened the first time, I tried to warn the guy that his family might not be okay with him dating me. And just like I did with Chad, I asked him if he had thought about x, y, and z.

"It will be fine," the guy scoffed, not fully taking into account the weight of what I was trying to get him to think about.

Sadly, it didn't take long for him to come to the conclusion that the pressure from his family was too much to bear and that it—or rather, *I*—was not worth it.

I didn't want this to happen again with Chad. I cared about him way too much—more than anyone I'd dated before—to run the risk of possibly hating him someday.

So, with tears rolling down my cheeks, my heart breaking, and my eyes still on the letter, I quietly said to him, "I think we need to break up."

C: Those words were crushing to hear. I understood why Adaeze made this declaration, but I wasn't willing to accept it. What we had was too good and so worth fighting for. We were only a couple of months in, but it was clear—to me, anyway—that what we had together was a good thing. So I grabbed her face and told her, "Adaeze, look at me." When she eventually did, I locked eyes with her and said, "I am not going anywhere. You are worth it. I want to be with you. I am not going to let any outside pressure come between us. I do not want this to break us up."

A: "I feel all those things toward you too," I croaked, attempting to sniffle back what now felt like tears coming out of my nose.

I do not cry cute.

"But I don't want to get in between you and your family. I need you to think about what this could do to your relationship with your family. And I need you to *really* think about it. Like, *actually* go take some time."

C: "I've already taken all the time I need to think about this," I assured her. "I just want you."

A: "Are you sure?" I pushed. "Are you sure you know what that means? I don't want you to get deeper into this and then realize it's way more than you signed up for and not worth the fight."

C: Adaeze was not making eye contact. She does that when she feels unsafe or vulnerable. I grabbed her face again.

"Adaeze Noelle Azubuike. Look at me for a second." I wanted those piercing, deep-brown eyes to meet mine.

When she finally, albeit hesitantly, looked at me, I said, "I'll be honest. I don't exactly know what this means. I have no way of knowing what this means. We have heard and dealt with this kind of stuff enough over the past two months for me to ask myself if I really want to continue moving forward. Every single time, I tell myself, *Adaeze is worth it.* So even though I don't know exactly what I am getting into, I'm telling you: I'm here to ride the wave with you. I know there will be trouble along the way, but I want to fight through it with you."

Still clutching her face, I promised her again, "I'm not going anywhere."

A: Still shaken from the letter, I couldn't bring myself to fully believe Chad in that moment.

I wanted to, though.

By faith and faith alone, I weakly replied, "Okay."

He pulled me in, and we held each other for a long time. With Chad's arms around me, the weight on my shoulders from reading the letter got a little lighter. Unlike the situation years prior with my ex, this time, I wasn't alone. For the first time in my dating life, I had finally found someone who thought I was worth the fight.

C & A: Receiving that letter was a make-it-or-break-it moment for us. Instead of breaking us up, it drove us closer together. Granted, a lot of other crap hit the fan after that—all of it coming from the outside—but that was the point when we actually started to believe that what we had with each other was worth it.

It was one of those "in the fire" moments that melded us together in the best way. We got to see how something that Satan meant for evil the Lord used for good by allowing it to draw us closer together (Genesis 50:20; Romans 8:28).

Because we both knew we were willing to fight for each other, whenever conversations about race came up, we were able to stay open and grow even closer. We learned how to feel with each other and appreciate the other person's perspective, and after we'd gone on an emotional journey together, to always come back to home base. We were committed to seeing each other as equals and believing that the path forward was *together*.

This isn't to say that you have to have a heartbreaking conflict or devastating event that almost breaks you in order to survive an interracial relationship—romantic or otherwise. But when difficult situations and conversations do arise (because they will) or you get frustrated that yet another issue is coming up (because it will), we hope you will remember that all of it has the potential to either end things between you or draw you closer together and make you stronger.

BEYOND WORDS

C: Spoiler alert . . . my family is in a totally different place now, and they have all grown a ton. The key, I think, was a conversation we had shortly after the big blowup over the letter. The gist of that conversation was, "We need to stop talking about the color of Adaeze's skin and start talking about *Adaeze*, the person."

Sure enough, once my parents started spending time with Adaeze, the walls began to come down, brick by brick.

I wouldn't say there was a particular moment when the switch flipped. Rather, what began the healing process was a collection of mundane moments that became treasured memories with real, loving people. It took time spent together to grow us into a family. It didn't just happen when Adaeze and I went to the altar.

A: During one phone call Chad and I had with his parents, my mother-in-love (yes, I really do call her that now) encouraged me, "Adaeze, sometimes in-law relationships just need time."

Slowly but surely, I started to see how right she was. It wasn't just calendar time but time spent with Chad's family that helped me let go of past pains and see the potential for healing. My pride told me that it was safer for me to constantly keep up my defenses with Chad's family, lest I suffer more pain at the hands of the people I so desperately wanted to accept me for me. But that's not how you grow closer to others.

Similar to the start of my relationship with Chad, I had to decide whether—deep down—I truly believed his family was worth the effort of trying with them, again and again. Even though I felt misunderstood. Even though I didn't always understand.

But because I love Chad, I also love his family, so they will always be worth the effort. I just had to learn how to establish a healthy balance between learning from past pain and remaining openhearted.

C: We still hit the occasional bump in the road, but hey, what families don't step on each other's toes from time to time? It was a rough start, but they genuinely love Adaeze and have happily accepted her as part of our family.

C&A: We'll talk a little more about how we bridged the gap between our families later on, but for now, the thing to remember is that overcoming past hurts and prejudices takes time. It takes patience. It takes understanding. And it takes a willingness to stay in the fight even if you get a little bruised and bloodied in the process, because meaningful relationships are inherently messy. Add in a racial dynamic that brings with it a well of hurt and emotion, and these dynamics can be a recipe for disaster. But they can also create a space where we are able to see the beauty of God's wonderfully diverse creation and stand in awe of a Creator who made us all different yet all in His image.

So be encouraged. These conversations can be uncomfortable and even painful, but if you truly care about each other and are willing to put in the time and the effort to learn and grow, we promise you it will be worth it.

CHAPTER 3

DOES EVERYTHING HAVE TO BE ABOUT RACE?

C: One day, when we'd been dating for about six months, Adaeze called. I assumed she was just checking in on her way to the gym, but I could tell from her voice that something was wrong. Her breathing was labored, and she was barely articulate.

Between staggered breaths, she told me she had been pulled over. I asked if the officer was still there.

"No. He gave me a ticket and left."

She was so upset, I asked her if something bad had happened during her interaction with the police officer, but she said it was just a routine traffic stop. Yet several moments after the officer had driven away, Adaeze was still parked on the side of the road, shaken and gasping for air.

I took a few deep breaths with her to help her calm down. "What's going on, Adaeze? Talk to me." I could still hear the panic in her voice as she said . . .

A: "I saw the flashing red and blue lights, and all I could think about was Jacob Blake and George Floyd . . ."

C: I knew exactly what she was talking about. A few weeks earlier, Jacob Blake had been shot seven times in the back by police officers in Kenosha, Wisconsin. The story had flooded news streams around the country. And this was right on the heels of George Floyd's death in Minneapolis, also at the hands of the police.

I suddenly realized how different an experience like this was for her than it was for me.

I've been pulled over before. Naturally, I was frustrated. Maybe a little annoyed that the officer decided to pull *me* over when the person in front of me was going much faster. At no point, though, was I worried about my safety.

In contrast, there was Adaeze, heart racing and wondering if she should grab her phone and try to livestream the whole thing on social media so someone could get help if anything went sideways.

I was thinking about insurance hikes, figuring out how I was going to pay the fine, and feeling angry at the police officer for doing his job. Adaeze was praying to God that she would not be the next national news story.

Later that night, I talked to a family member on the phone.

"You have to understand," I explained, "Adaeze's world is just different. When she sees police lights in her rearview mirror, she's legit wondering if she's going to be the next victim of police violence."

"What does race have to do with it?" came the retort. "You just need to learn to respect the authorities." The implication being that if something bad had happened to Adaeze, it would have been because she didn't know how to respect others. This couldn't have been further from the truth.

Then they said, "There just needs to be strong father figures to teach these things."

Now that cut deep. To assume that Adaeze was a disrespectful person who couldn't handle herself with authorities was not only completely false—it was a degradation of her character. But to take it a step further and say that all Black fathers are failing not only their kids but society?

That gross generalization of an entire community is steeped in historically biased bigotry and leaves no room for any other statement to be considered truth.

Adaeze lost her dad in 2010, yet his influence on her is still so strong that it is almost futile to try to put it into words. This man, whom I never had the pleasure to meet, oozes through his daughter. His kindness and gracious heart shine through her. His love of the Word, his wisdom, and his consistent devotion to Jesus live on through her. And his infectious spirit continues to make waves because of the kind of friend and leader Adaeze is.

Regardless, pinning the blame on Black fathers is gaslighting at its finest. It says that the actions of a dangerously biased white officer do not matter, and it places the fault on the shoulders of the Black father, no matter the quality of his parenting.

"This has nothing to do with father figures," I said, trying to keep the edge out of my voice. "Adaeze had an amazing father and mother who taught her how to respect others, including authorities. Here's what you're missing: when Adaeze sees shootings and violence on TV, she sees her brothers. She sees herself."

"But as long as she doesn't do anything wrong . . ." they countered.

"It doesn't always matter," I cut in. "Look at Ahmaud Arbery. He was just out jogging in Georgia, and a couple of white guys in a pickup chased him down and killed him with shotguns. He wasn't doing anything wrong. He was just minding his own business, and the next thing you know, he's a victim. When the police showed up, they didn't do anything. Those guys killed an innocent man, and nobody got arrested or was held accountable until months later when a video of the shooting went viral. So, when Adaeze sees police lights behind her, she's hoping that whoever gets out of that vehicle isn't corrupt. She also does everything in her power to show that person as much respect as she can to make sure they have no reason whatsoever to think she might be a threat. Out of self-preservation, she has to think about things differently than you or I would."

A: When Chad told me about this conversation, it wasn't the first time I'd heard the idea that Black people just need to learn to behave. Unfortunately, instead of leaning toward compassion and empathy, Chad's family member immediately assumed the worst of me and all Black people. The root of the issue is the assumption that any problem in an interracial interaction is the fault of the person of color. This is why, early on, I had a difficult time moving forward in love with this particular family member. It seemed like no matter where I was coming from, they didn't wanna hear about my experiences. In their mind, I was in the wrong and the white person was right.

This is damaging for interracial relationships because when we enter into them with this bent toward white people being the moral default, we assume the problem must lie with whoever is not them. Conversely, that means Black people typically fall under the default of villainy, no matter our actions.

Under this scope, even when a Black person acts respectful when pulled over and has their hands on the ten and two and says, "Yes, sir," or "No, ma'am," sometimes it's not enough. Society usually defaults to the good intentions of white people as a whole rather than acknowledging the good intentions of Black people as a whole. This is why Black people can often feel like we have to walk on eggshells around white people—always on our best behavior so we don't fulfill a negative stereotype that has been wrongfully placed on us.

C: As white people, we can feel like we need to walk on eggshells as well. The difference is that our anxiety is self-inflicted. Adaeze feels pressured by white society to act a certain way. I, on the other hand, become stifled because I expect perfection from a Black person, and when they do not meet it, I label them an angry Black person. We both backpedal, but in my case, it's out of fear of facing the wrath of the stereotype I just created in my head. The Black person steps back in an attempt to dodge the familiar label they see waiting to jump onto them like a persistent nemesis.

By the way, lest you think situations like Jacob Blake or George Floyd are isolated incidents, not long ago, a Black friend of ours from church was visiting his parents in Arizona. One night, he was driving back to their house around 10:00 p.m., when he saw red and blue flashing lights. He pulled over.

The police officer came up to his window and asked him to get out of the vehicle. He was not told why he'd been pulled over, so our friend asked the officer for an explanation before he got out of the car.

Just to be clear, he had not been speeding and was not

offered any information, nor was he asked for his license and registration. He was just immediately asked to get out of the car.

When our friend instead asked a question, the cop pulled his gun on him. Then, with a barrel pointed at his head, our friend got out of his car and was handcuffed on the hood. The officer proceeded to search his vehicle. Of course, he found nothing.

A: Every time I think of this story, I'm so thankful to God that this police officer didn't plant a small baggie of drugs as he searched our friend's vehicle. This is a tired trick that, sadly, the Black community has heard of too many times.

C: As the officer uncuffed him, he gave our friend a warning that he should not be driving around this neighborhood (which happened to be a wealthy, predominantly white neighborhood) that late at night. In the end, the officer left without doing anything other than severely racially profiling a young man down the road from his parents' house.

This type of thing happens to Black people all the time.

The fact that my family member was unable to fathom what race had to do with Adaeze's "routine traffic stop" underscored how oblivious they were to the fact that people with a different skin color live in a completely different reality than white people do.

If we're being totally honest, most white people (myself included) have probably asked that same "What does race have to do with it?" question before. But before we write off Adaeze's response to a traffic stop as a case of paranoia or oversensitivity, let me share a few incidents that made me realize just how often things *are* about race.

"ARE YOU TWO . . . *TOGETHER*?"

C: One evening, shortly after we were married, Adaeze and I were hanging out at a distillery near our home. This place was tiny— I mean, *really* tiny. Packed to capacity, it can probably hold fifteen customers, tops. As it happened, on this particular night, we were the only customers in the place and had been for the better part of an hour.

We'd both had a rough day and were kicking back in a corner booth, enjoying some much-needed time together and having a drink or two to unwind. The whole time we were there, we were talking, laughing, and hanging all over each other. We were also in close enough proximity to the bartender to pull her into our conversation a handful of times because it almost felt awkward if we didn't.

When it started getting late, Adaeze and I asked for the check. The white female bartender—who had been right there watching us and listening to our conversation—walked over and asked, "Is the check together or separate?"

A: Okay, you might be wondering, *So what does that have to do with race?* If that were an isolated incident, maybe we could write it off, but after it's happened enough times, it's hard to deny the trend. Here's another story from early on in our marriage for you.

We were in a grocery store, joking, laughing, and taking turns grabbing what we needed off the shelves. Don't ask me why, but for some reason, whenever Chad and I go to the grocery store, we never get a cart, regardless of how much stuff we need. We just grab one of those little hand-held baskets, which Chad, being the gentleman he is, always insists on carrying. And I am more than happy to oblige.

On this particular trip, our grocery selection went far beyond the capacity of our basket to the point that both our arms were completely full.

C: And that was before we realized we also needed milk . . .

A: And paper towels.

C: Yeah, we had not thought this through.

A: We were still cracking up as we walked up to the checkout. Chad was in front of me, having just made some goofy comment that got me cackling pretty good. The cashier was standing behind one of those cash registers that doesn't have a grocery belt and only has a little counter where you can set your stuff down. Chad put our basket down, still very much interacting with me, and I with him. Because the counter was full, I waited to hand the white male cashier the rest of our groceries until after he emptied the basket so as to not overwhelm him with too much at once.

Then, as I started to hand him the paper towels, he literally put two hands up toward me as if to say, "Whoa . . . wait a minute." He looked at Chad and asked, "Is this all together?" as if I was trying to sneak my own personal groceries onto Chad's bill or something.

We were both floored.

C: I mean, think about it. When was the last time you were asked, "Together or separate?" at a *grocery store*? It just doesn't happen. Why? Because it is so incredibly clear when people are checking out together—especially when you're standing together in a space the size of an airplane bathroom . . .

A: Aaand the other person literally hands you more groceries as you're scanning the first person's stuff. So we *both* said . . .

C & A: "Uh, yeah, it's together . . ."

A: Which was enough to send the guy into major backpedal mode. Still facing me, he kept his hands up in defense, as if I'd just asked him to empty the cash register for me. The way he was looking at me almost seemed like he wanted me to prove that I was married to Chad, even though my wedding ring (which Chad had custom-made for me, by the way) was facing him as I held the paper towels. Completely exasperated, I looked over at Chad, who was staring—dumbfounded—at the cashier.

"Okay," the cashier said defensively, with his hands up in a let's-all-take-it-easy-here kind of way. "I just wanted to make sure." It was almost as though he was trying to convince us he was just doing his job.

C: Which was a bunch of bull.

A: I was sooo close to asking him, "Do you ask every customer that?" But I bit my tongue. Sometimes the fruit of the Spirit, namely self-control, actually does win out in me.

C: Anyway, we paid for our groceries and walked out of the store, and as we walked to the car, we just stared at each other, perplexed.

A: We finally broke the silence and asked each other, in unison, "Did he *really* just ask us that?"

C: This has happened to us so many times, in a variety of circumstances.

A: And it's not just us—some of our friends have noticed it too.

C: One time, we were on a double date with a white couple. When the waiter was ready to bring out the checks, he pointed Adaeze and me out and asked if we were together or separate. He did not, however, ask our friends the same question.

A: Picture it. Chad and I were sitting together on one side of the table, and our friends were sitting together on the other side. The point being: there were clearly two couples present, but only we—the interracial couple—were asked how we wanted to handle the check.

C: After enough incidents like this, you reach a point where you realize this likely never would have happened were we not an interracial couple.

A: This is why the question, "What does this have to do with race?" has to be genuinely considered by the person asking— not in an exasperated way but from a truly reflective place. This question arises not only in everyday situations like these but also in situations that feel particularly triggering.

C: Like when you got pulled over in the wake of George Floyd, Ahmaud Arbery, and Jacob Blake.

A: Exactly. In fact, when we were driving from Asheville to Durham to visit some friends—on the same day we saw those two guys walking around wearing camo and Confederate flag gear—we drove right past the biggest Confederate flag I have ever seen. It was right there on the side of the road, waving proudly in the wind, looming over the highway. If I didn't know better, I'da sworn that thing was saying, "Get outta here"—directly to me.

C: As oblivious as I'd been during that trip, I *did* notice that Adaeze was upset by it. (Well done, Chad.) So I reached over, took her hand, and said, "You know . . . the Confederate flag is also about showing Southern pride. It's not *just* about racism." (Well done, Chad—retrospective facepalm.)

A: My man.

C: I know. I'm sorry. Poor timing.

A: Actually, what Chad said wasn't untrue. The Confederate flag *is* a symbol of Southern pride. What initially bothered me about Chad's comment was the implication that because the flag also represents Southern pride, I shouldn't be bothered by its association with racism—as if one naturally cancels out the other. In other words, my feelings were invalid because, "Look what else is true."

The problem with a white person making a statement like this is that it absolves them from having to sit in the pain of the situation with the person of color. It's like they're subconsciously saying, "Yeah . . . I really don't wanna deal with this, so here's what I'm gonna offer you." They acknowledge it, but they don't own it. It's a consolation prize—a "there, there" that doesn't help the recipient at all but makes the sender feel good about themselves for having made the effort.

SOMETIMES IT'S NOT ABOUT RACE

C: Okay, now that we've talked about how much race plays into things, we should probably mention one area where it doesn't—at least not for us.

So many people look at our relationship as difficult purely because I am white and Adaeze is Black. Sure, cultural differences make things difficult at times, but my life is not harder because of my wife's skin color, nor is hers harder because of mine.

The truth is a lot of relationships have problems that are not visible, at least not immediately.

For example, a colleague might have a history of alcoholism in their family and not want to go out for happy hour with the team.

Two friends may have grown up on opposite sides of the financial tracks and have opposing views about how to handle money at a bachelor party.

One roommate might come from a family that talks everything out and embraces healthy conflict, while the other comes from a family where speaking one's mind was considered talking back and everything was swept under the rug for the sake of keeping a faux sense of peace.

These are all factors that cause issues in relationships, but because you can't see them, most people don't ask about them. Race, however, is a visible "problem," which gets inflated to seem much more serious than a lot of the unseen, "normal" problems in relationships.

It's fascinating to me that people will come up to Adaeze or me, or both of us together, and ask, "What's it like to be in an interracial marriage?" But nobody ever walks up to anyone and asks, "What's it like to be friends with someone who grew up so much richer (or poorer) than you?" Or "What's it like working with someone who grew up in Texas when you're from the Bronx?"

I wonder what makes people feel like they even have a right to ask that kind of question. What is it about race that seems to give a free pass to dig into someone else's private business?

A: We are not naive enough to think that being Black and white in a relationship doesn't bring its own set of unique challenges. We could write a book about that.

C: We have!

A: Ha! (We clever.) We could probably write another one because we live in a world that all too often tells us—in one way or another—that we're too different from each other to make this work.

Ironically, most of the issues that do arise as a result of us being an interracial couple originate from *outside* our relationship. Other people may have a problem with it, but me and Chad? We geuh.

C: That's why we wish the people who don't understand or approve of our relationship could see from the inside how good it is instead of looking at it from the outside through their own filters.

CHAPTER 4

UNDER THE INFLUENCE

C: About two months into our relationship, Adaeze and I were starting to get serious, so we officially had the DTR (define the relationship) conversation. I thought I was giving hints about our relationship status by asking Adaeze things like "So we're dating, right?"

To which Adaeze would respond with something like "Yes, we're going on dates right now."

A: My three older brothers would have been so proud of me in that moment. I didn't assume anything Chad *wasn't* saying, because my brothers had taught me: "If the guy doesn't call it a date, it's not a date." And "If the guy doesn't ask you to be his girl, you ain't his girl!" I was taking zero chances with this one.

C: I tried again with other words.

Relationship.

Going out.

Together.

Courting?

Finally, I understood. I needed to say the word *girlfriend*. So I specifically asked, "Adaeze, will you be my girlfriend?"

A: "Of course, why didn't you just ask that?" (Fellas, it's just nice to be asked.)

C: Aaanyway, as our relationship continued to move forward, we dove deeper into unchartered territory for both of us. We were past figuring each other out and now moving into the stage where we were hiding less and less from each other.

One day, we sat on the couch to relax for a little bit. We had been talking about TV shows that only one of us had seen, and I picked out one that I loved and wanted to share with her.

This was in the fall of 2020, in the wake of the racial tension that had taken place that summer. Adaeze, like much of the country, was still grieving and trying to process it all. After I turned on the show, she looked at me and asked, "Can we please watch something with at least *one* Black person in it?"

I hadn't even thought about it until she mentioned it, but she was right. The primary cast was all white. Admittedly, my gut reaction was to say, *Can't you just enjoy a good show?* and *Didn't you just see that Black person on the screen?* and point out the one Black extra in a sea of whiteness.

Thank You, Jesus, that I did not vocalize either thought. Instead, I simply said, "Yeah, of course. Let's find something else." I began searching for a show that had a Black main character. After about five minutes of scrolling, I finally gave up. I could not find a single show that was not led by a white character. Prior to that moment, I'd had no idea how extreme the lack of representation was in our culture.

A: For the record, it wasn't necessarily bad that Chad hadn't been watching shows with a Black lead. It was just disheartening that he had to try so hard to find one. I could blame his streaming service for not suggesting more diverse shows or chalk it up to his search history. However, when you compare his futile search for a Black lead with how often white people see themselves represented on TV and in film, there's really no argument to be made about the discrepancy. It's painfully obvious.

Even the term "Black show" seems sadly necessary because it is such an anomaly. To me, the term is kind of redundant. So is Black History Month. It's just "history month" to me. Or like Black Friday . . .

C: Nope.

A: Tee-hee.

It was a very different world in the US before 2020, which is when the entertainment industry slowly began to wake up to how noninclusive its representation was. At least now, more shows have people of color in them and feature interracial couples. We're even seeing diversity in luxury vehicle commercials. It's awesome!

But that day on the couch with Chad, the TV listings were like a microcosm of what I was experiencing on a broader scale. Everything that had happened that summer—the racially motivated murders—was still fresh, and I was emotionally exhausted.

At the end of a long workday in a white space, I just wanted to see something familiar that wouldn't make me feel "othered." And Chad's pull-up of another white-male-dominated show was enough for me to finally ask for what I needed and not feel ashamed to ask for it (though I did feel a bit sheepish).

I didn't want to make him feel guilty for not having thought to select a show with that criterion. I mean, why would he have, before being with me?

When I spoke up, I was reteaching myself that it's not a bad thing to want to see myself represented on the media box Chad and I stared at most evenings—especially since the COVID-19 stay-at-home orders meant I wasn't able to hang with my friends. I just needed to feel some sense of Black community—even if it was only on TV.

C: To Adaeze's point, you could try to blame the lack of diverse representation on my streaming algorithm. Or you could say, "Of course, my entertainment is white. Look at the lack of diversity in Hollywood!" (This is definitely an argument I've used in the past.) Even now, when I play music at work, I try to select stations based on the names of Black artists, but my streaming service likes to sprinkle in other Black artists who do not fall under the same musical genre. For example, I can choose a Leon Bridges station, expecting chill, R & B/soul type of music, which would be appropriate for a physical therapy clinic. But inevitably, I have to change the station after my first couple of patients because, out of nowhere, artists with explicit rap lyrics will start playing. And believe me, Childish Gambino and Drake don't sit well with a seventy-five-year-old grandma named Gertrude.

However, if I pick an Allen Stone station, I get the smooth

R & B/soul music I'm attempting to play. (In case you don't know, Allen Stone is a white guy and Leon Bridges is a Black guy. Their music is fairly similar, but somehow, in an algorithm, they are placed into racially separate categories, and Leon Bridges ends up in the "urban music" category.)

A: In other words, music-streaming companies have mostly defined Black music as vulgar rap. And hey, if that is your jam, then you do you. But that's not *all* Black music is. This is what happens when people who attempt to define Blackness are not Black.

Speaking of the word *Black* . . .

I'm aware that the term *Black* can be triggering for some Black people, especially those who connect the origin of that term with the term *Negro*, noting that both were used as a way to dehumanize those of African descent. There can be hesitation to even utter the term *Black* because it's seen as negative. For a number of years, *African American* was used as an alternative and somehow believed to be more culturally appropriate. But this presumes that all Black people identify as such. What about all the Caribbean Americans, for example, who are completely glossed over with that term?

My suggestion would be to simply ask people what term they prefer instead of making broad assumptions. When we put labels on others who are different from us, instead of actually getting to know them and learning about them, we run the risk of hurting them and incorrectly and negatively influencing others around us about that race.

C: That is exactly why it is so important—especially as a white person—to seek out influences of other races. Otherwise, we are at the mercy of the algorithms.

Speaking of which, not long after the TV show debacle, we were in my car listening to some music on my streaming service, and Adaeze asked me . . .

A: "Do you listen to any Black artists?"

C: "Of course I do!"

Confident that I would find plenty of non-white artists in my library, I grabbed my phone and started scrolling through my saved list. I was fully expecting to be inundated with an array of skin tones representing my musical taste.

I made it all the way to *G* before I found one.

"There, Gary Clark Jr.!" I exclaimed.

But much like with the "Beyoncé effect," I knew that rattling off one incredible and well-known guitar player would not suffice. So I continued scrolling.

And scrolling.

And scrolling.

And 100 percent serious: Gary Clark Jr. was the only Black artist in my entire library. I didn't even have a random Beyoncé song in there.

Then Adaeze asked me . . .

A: "Are there any *female* artists in your library?"

C: Sadly, the exact same thing happened.

Sorry, women of music.

The point is—unless we make a conscious effort to introduce some diversity into our television, film, or music library—algorithms will keep us squarely within our comfort zones. Our stereotypes are created by our spheres of exposure. The algorithms filter everything else out and keep us safely—and ignorantly—within a little white bubble.

IT AIN'T *ALL* ABOUT ALGORITHMS

A: When we first started dating, I wanted to learn all about Chad, specifically his history with Black culture. One day, we were talking about our friends. I thought about the fact that most of Chad's close friends—at least the ones I had met—were white. That wasn't necessarily a bad thing. I honestly assumed he did have Black friends, and I wanted to meet them.

So I casually asked, "Besides me, do you hang out with other Black people?"

C: But what I heard was, *You ignorant racist white boy. You don't have a single Black friend, and you're trying to date me?*

Now, clearly, that was *not* what Adaeze said or was implying, yet I immediately went on the defensive. "What do you mean, do I have Black friends?"

A: "Umm, like . . . do you have . . . any close friends . . . who are Black?"

I didn't know what else to say. I thought it was a very clear question.

C: "I had a Black friend in college."

Yeah, I was totally grasping at straws. And I felt triggered. So naturally, I lashed out. "I feel like you're coming at me because I don't have enough Black friends for you."

A: "It's not that. You pretty much just said you don't have any Black friends, which is interesting to me. I'm not saying there's anything wrong with having white friends. I just find the fact that I am the only Black person in your life . . . umm . . . interesting."

C: "I just haven't had many opportunities to be friends with Black people."

A: "Okay."

C: "I mean, I try. But what do you expect? There are no Black people around us! I live in Colorado!"

A: *Dear Lord, help me today.*

For the record, I have heard the whole "No Black people live around me" defense so many times from well-intentioned white friends.

"Adaeze," they say, "I wanna diversify my circle, but no Black people live around me. What can I do?"

Once again, it comes down to intentionality. Just like blaming an algorithm for not automatically introducing Black artists into your library, you can't put all the onus on Black people to move into your area so you can diversify your life.

If you've felt that way, here's what I would lovingly challenge you to do: think of it the other way around. Instead of saying, "There are no Black people near me," say to yourself, *I am not around Black people. I am not around people of color.* This makes it easier to do something about it.

Google Black-owned restaurants and suggest those spots when you and a friend are figuring out where to grab lunch or you're looking for a fun place to go on date night. Don't just go to a Mexican restaurant for the delicious food. Meet the owner while you're there. If you can, ask your server if you may converse with him or her in Spanish, and try to learn something new from your visit. Learn the names of the people of color who own small businesses and support them.

Diversifying your life does not depend on anyone else but you. Instead of using where you live as an excuse, broaden your circle a little. You might be pleasantly surprised.

C: I'll even go one step further. Unless you live in one of the few places in the United States that is 97 percent white, odds are you know at least a couple of people of color who are close enough to you that you go out for a beer together. The church that Adaeze and I met at is megawhite, but even in my small circle, there were three or four guys I could have tried to get closer to. I just didn't ask. I chose not to reach out. Was this because of their skin color? I don't think so—not deliberately, anyway. But subconsciously, that may have had something to do with it. Sadly, these guys didn't make it onto my priority list because my white culture told me that our compatibility would be lower than mine with the white person standing next to them.

So, yes, we can diversify by broadening our circles. However, odds are, you are neglecting a person of color who is already within your current circle.

A: Preach, baby!

GET OUT THERE

C & A: There's no question that the media and our culture at large shape not only the way we see people but the type of people we see. That's why we need to actively seek out and lean into spaces where we can collide with people who are different from us.

It's a start to go to places like restaurants, bars, dance studios, and gyms frequented or owned by people who do not look like you. However, you might also consider taking in a concert featuring a band you don't normally listen to or going to an ethnically diverse museum exhibit, film festival, or craft fair. Or you might simply invite your Black coworker, classmate, or neighbor out for coffee or lunch.

If you're a Christian, you might consider visiting a multicultural church. Multicultural churches are beautiful because they provide us with the opportunity to grow as a unified people under the Name of Jesus. That is how it will be when people from every nation, tribe, and language bow before the throne of God (Revelation 7).

Whatever steps you take, we think you'll find that simply being in the presence of a multitude of cultures and skin tones will help you see past the stereotypes and separate the truth from the negative influences that have kept us at arm's length from one another.

The more familiar we are with someone's history and reality, the less likely we are to butt heads, dismiss them, offend them, or inadvertently say or do something that hurts or excludes them. The best way to gain familiarity with each other is to . . . wait for it . . . spend time together!

CHAPTER 5

EXCUSE ME, BUT I THINK YOU JUST STEPPED IN SOMETHING

A: How do you lovingly say no when someone asks to touch your hair?

I instinctively winced at my friend's text. She continued,

It happened at work today, and of course I froze and then just said yes.

She ended the text with a facepalm emoji for emphasis.

Ahh noooooooooo! I'm so sorry to hear this happened to you.

I texted back with a few line-eyed emojis (you know, the one that conveys ultimate frustration), along with the emoji signaling that a bad word is being bleeped out.

WHITE BOY / BLACK GIRL

I wanted to understand where she was coming from before answering her question, so I asked why she felt the burden to say something other than no. She texted back,

I think it's because I know her. She's a sweet older white lady, and I know she was well-intentioned. I think I got worried about the aftermath (awkwardness, hurt feelings, etc.) and wanted to avoid that. [Shrug emoji.]

Eventually the conversation became involved enough that we abandoned texting and started sending voice messages back and forth. One of the biggest things that came out of the conversation, for both of us, was the realization that we Black women do exactly what my friend did—a lot. We assume it's gonna be awkward—for us, the white person, or both—if we say, "No, I don't want you to touch my hair." So, at our own expense, we default to protecting the feelings of the white person.

We do this all the time—put ourselves second—to "keep the peace" because that's what we've been incorrectly taught peace means. This may divert awkwardness in the moment, but it turns into a dysfunctional cycle. A white person does something borderline offensive, and we don't want to offend them back, so we absorb all the uncomfortableness. To spare their feelings, we tell them, "It's okay." Then we walk away frustrated at the world for being the way it is, when all we've done is perpetuate the problem. This vicious cycle is repeated again and again, which only adds to our jaded view of the world and of white people.

We don't really know how people will respond if we tell them the truth. Maybe it will be awkward. Maybe it won't. Maybe the white person *will* have hurt feelings. But even if they do, is that our fault? We were simply answering their question honestly.

One of the things I reminded my friend of in the conversation was, "You did not ask for this, so keep your peace! Speak your preference. If you say no and she's offended, it's not your responsibility. And you don't need to explain your preference if you don't want to. A simple 'No, thank you' suffices just fine, because 'No' is a full sentence. If anything, it reminds her that you're allowed to say no. If she asks why and you want to elaborate, that's up to you, not her."

WHAT'S THE BIG DEAL?

C: The first time Adaeze told me a story about someone touching her hair, I didn't get it at all.

When I was a kid, people would run their fingers through my hair and comment on how spiky it was, and sometimes older people would touch my head as a form of endearment. I didn't see why it was such a big deal.

My gut reaction was to ask her why she was getting so defensive over something so small. I mean, the offender was just trying to show interest in her.

I asked her, "Babe, why does it bother you so much to have someone touch your hair?" (Can you hear the subtle condescension of that question?)

A: "Because I don't *want* my hair touched. It's rude and othering. But it goes much deeper than that. For one thing, it's my body. So it shouldn't have to be explained why I don't want someone touching part of my body, especially without my permission, even if it's well-intentioned. The fact that we're having this discussion and that this is such a constant subject for Black women especially baffles me. The conversation could just stop at our preference for not wanting our hair touched, yet we always seem to have to explain why. When this happens, it's usually about what the white person wants. Their desire is based on curiosity, not on me as a human being. I mean, think about that question: *Can I touch your hair?* Have you ever heard someone ask that to a white woman with straight blond hair? Why is it being asked of me? Because my hair is 'different'? So now because I'm seen as different to someone, I have to deal with wanting to be touched in order to be understood? That's so weird! That makes no sense!"

C: "But they're curious, and they're not used to seeing Black women's hair. Your personal boundaries need to be respected, for sure, but isn't it a good thing that they're trying to learn?"

A: "The problem isn't that they wanna learn more. It's the implied diminishment that comes with it. Beyond showing disrespect for my personal boundaries, the question itself carries an entitled attitude of, 'I'm curious, I want to touch your hair, and you should fall under that and be okay with it.' When we say no, most of the time the asker takes offense, as if they own my personal and emotional space.

"So it's not so much the intent, even if it's meant to compliment me. It's where the question is rooted and the way it makes me feel. That's the unfortunate mind game of it. If I say yes, the white person gets to be the innocent, curious, wanting-to-learn one who walks away none the wiser and completely unaffected. I'm left having to go above and beyond, yet again, because I'm different from the majority. I'm expected to continually look past any personal offense because they 'just want to learn about me' or they're 'just curious.' Over and over. It's exhausting. Whether they realize it or not, it's rooted in racism or prejudice."

C: I kept trying to encourage Adaeze to take it as a compliment. She kept trying to explain to me how uncomfortable it could be for people to ask about or try to touch her hair. By the end of the conversation, I still didn't fully understand. What's more, I had a difficult time classifying the hair situation as racism or prejudice.

So I asked, "What part of touching or asking about your hair looks like racism to you?" You may have read that with a caring inflection from me, but if I'm being honest, it was closer to the tone of, *I'm going to win this argument.*

A: "It's not always specific racism. Sometimes it's more of a microaggression—a subtle or not-so-subtle act of discrimination, usually from people who aren't trying to be overtly racist. And by microaggression, I mean something the receiver often feels like they're not allowed to be upset about because it seems so small to everyone else. Like the things society would say you're overreacting to if you speak up about them. The things people imply you're being dramatic about and are often met with, 'Can't you take a joke?' or, 'Don't take everything so seriously.'"

C: Okay, let's hit pause for a second because something is playing out here that needs a little extra backstory.

For a while, it was difficult for me to engage in racial conversations with Adaeze because I felt like even with the best of intentions, I would invariably hit a land mine. I never wanted to upset her, but sometimes in my attempt to take an interest in her, it felt like I did just that. She would be offended, I imme-diately put walls up, and the conversation fell flat soon after it took off.

Eventually, I started to shy away because I felt like I had to do everything correctly. When an intense conversation started, I would be so timid that I had basically already begun my Nick Miller moonwalk out of the room. (If you missed the reference, go watch *New Girl*.)

This led to an increased defensiveness toward Adaeze when she talked about having to "protect white people's feelings," to the point that my own insecurity made me more difficult to talk to. Before I knew it, I became the white man whose feelings Adaeze felt she had to protect.

That's what was happening here. I got so defensive about not wanting to be perceived as a racist white dude that as soon as Adaeze tried to explain her point of view, instead of really listening and hearing her, I made her totally valid perspective the problem. In doing so, I was gaslighting her in her frustra-tion with people touching her hair.

But thanks to Adaeze's thoughtful response, I was able to see what I was doing.

I reframed my question: "I'm getting the sense that there are deeper contextual meanings surrounding your hair. What are some of those?"

A: "I'm glad you asked!"

What Chad just asked was much more appropriate than the woman's question "Can I touch your hair?" One question humanizes me. The other does not. One is seeking to learn more about me. The other is all about satisfying the other person's curiosity. A lot of times, those kinds of questions don't leave room for the response to be no.

It's like walking up to a pregnant woman you don't know and asking if you can touch her stomach. Or worse, putting your hands on her belly, as if it's somehow your right to do so. Even if the question is asked—which my pregnant friends tell me it usually is not—how exactly is that interaction going to play out?

"Ooh . . . may I touch your belly?"

"Um, no, thank you."

"Oh . . ."

[Awkward silence.]

It's weird! It's uncomfortable! And it makes zero sense. But it happens all the time. In this case, it has nothing to do with racism—it's just a question of people lacking social awareness. And, sure, some Black people may not mind their hair being touched, but that should not be the rule. Nor should I be labeled overly sensitive if it's my preference for random people to not touch my hair.

The bottom line, whether it is a Black person's hair or a pregnant woman's belly, is that putting your hands on any part of someone else's body without their permission is inappropriate, period. It is not someone's right to touch you just because they want to. Asking the question, "Can I touch this?" only serves the purpose of satisfying one person's curiosity at the expense of the other.

Chad hit the nail on the head when he alluded to the fact that it's not just about my hair or about my personal history. Dating back to slavery, there's history of Black people's bodies being judged, objectified, and othered.

Also, historically, my 4C coiled hair hasn't been seen as a sign of beauty within mainstream media. The representation of my hair on major media—in a protective hairstyle like braids or locs—has been few and far between. So it makes sense that many "curious" white people haven't seen hair like mine before.

Sometimes I do appreciate people wanting to learn and asking genuine questions, if we're at a point in our relationship that warrants those kinds of personal conversations, instead of asking to touch my hair. However, it's objectifying to point out that my hair is "different," because here's the thing: Black hair isn't different for me. My hair is empowering to me. My hair is an integral part of my cultural experience. My hair has a history of being told that it needs to change to be acceptable or to be considered "professional."

Furthermore, the history of my hair goes back to when our ancestors braided theirs to keep it out of their faces while doing slave work. Maps to freedom were hidden within the different patterns of their creative hairstyles. After slavery was abolished, success was—unfortunately—defined by the white narrative. So initially, straightening our hair was a way to assimilate. Fast-forward to present day, and we Black women are starting to reclaim our hair. If we wanna bawse it sleek and straight, it doesn't mean there's assimilation happening—it's just a way to freely express ourselves. Rather than hiding directions to freedom, our braids and other hairstyles are works of art that we freely choose, encompassing all different textures, lengths, and colors.

Whether we're wearing our hair in kinky twists, crochet goddess locs, or au naturel in tight curls, it's beautiful, because it's us. It's uniquely our own. It's a revolutionary act of reclaiming not only our hair's worth but our own.

At the risk of sounding harsh, when a white person puts

their hands on my hair, possibly to satisfy a subconscious curiosity about what they see as "exotic" or "different," it's not only dishonoring to my hair's history and beauty—it's also demeaning. And small-minded. My hair's legacy is sacred to me and shouldn't be subjected to someone else's curiosity.

As for the whole "Just wanting to compliment you" excuse . . . it's tough because I know some people are coming from a place of good intentions and all that. But I'll be bold enough to say this for myself: touching my hair is the wrong way to compliment me.

As I write this, I have my hair in a "bun hawk," as I call it—a row of buns in the shape of a mohawk. This style could also be called Bantu knots, although that's typically more of an all-over-the-head style.

One of the first times I wore my hair like this—and I worked hard on it—someone in the lobby at church reached for my hair. I actually dodged their touch and said with a smile, "Nope, please don't touch it," while gently pushing their hand away. They reacted fine, and it wasn't a big deal, which gave me more confidence to continue speaking up before I'm touched in a way I don't approve of, not just after the fact.

It's not a compliment to me to be treated like something to be petted, even if it's meant in a good way. Aside from that, my hair look geuh! Don't mess it up! On a purely practical level, this is a reason not to touch someone's hair. They may have put a lot of time and effort into it. So sticking your fingers in it? Dass just rude. And touching their hair uninvited, with an "I've never seen one of these before" look on your face? That's not complimentary—it's othering. And it perpetuates the message that our hair is unappealing to general society, which in turn communicates an implied inferiority of Black women.

This is just part of why touching my hair goes so much deeper than it might seem on the surface. Yet there's rarely enough time or space between someone noticing my hair and reaching out to touch it for me to explain that. So while touching my hair or asking to touch it might not be a big deal to a white person, it could be the final nudge that pushes me over the edge, no matter how good the intention. They don't know my reality, and they don't typically pause to think about it before asking to invade my personal and emotional space.

So if you're in doubt, just stick to verbal compliments about someone's Black hair. You don't need to add physical touch to it.

And if you do decide to ask a Black woman about her hair, remember that your curiosity does not automatically entitle you to an answer. The expectation placed on Black women to educate white people gets very tiring. Sometimes we just done talking about it, like, *Can't I just be me without having to explain it to white people all the time?*

C: By the way, fellow white readers, I know my wife well, and as we are discussing this, I can tell she's trying hard to soften the blow despite this being a difficult topic. So, if you are feeling a little on the defensive right now, it might be because you see a little bit of yourself in this conversation. Don't worry—I've seen the less enlightened parts of myself in a lot of our conversations too. And you know what? That's a good thing! That means we're learning. We're becoming more aware of the cultural context that makes those "well-intentioned" comments or questions land wrong.

That's why Adaeze and I are writing this book—to hold up a mirror and help all of us see some of the blind spots that get in the way of healthy relationships with people who don't look like us.

C & A: In the spirit of holding up that sometimes-painful-but-necessary-if-we-really-want-to-grow-and-have-healthier-relationships mirror, let's talk about a few other microaggressions that may seem harmless but can actually be quite painful.

Again—and we can't emphasize this enough—our goal here is not to insult, attack, or offend anyone. The cold, hard truth is the things we're about to talk about have been insulting people of color for years, and if we want to avoid causing further damage, we need to understand why these comments, assumptions, and stereotypes are so harmful.

DID YOU REALLY JUST SAY THAT?

A: One of the most annoying microaggressions I've ever experienced was when a white male photographer told me, "You sound white."

We had just finished doing a photoshoot, and he was talking about my voice onstage—particularly when I was speaking to our congregation at the close of one of our live-album recordings.

The sad part? He was trying to compliment me.

When I confronted him about it, he tried to backpedal by saying, "That's not how I meant it."

Then what *was* the compliment he was intending to give me? That I speak well? That I sound intelligent?

Thankfully, he eventually apologized and said, "That was really ignorant."

Still, the fact that he said those three words as a compliment was not just a microaggression. It was an insult. It implied that if anything I did onstage sounded good, it was because I sounded like someone of another race, specifically a white person. It implied that Black people typically sound the opposite of good, intelligent, or some other fill-in-the-blank that makes people of color sound less than. Likewise, it insinuated that speaking well, intelligently, or confidently is inherently a "white person thing," as if white people somehow own speaking well and sounding intelligent. Even our own voices can't be ours!

C: In a similar way, when people make statements to Adaeze like, "Man, you're really pretty for a Black woman," they think they're paying her a compliment, but the implication is incredibly degrading—that it's surprising for a Black woman to be attractive. I mean, come on . . . have you *seen* my wife? She's freaking gorgeous!

A: Awww, thank you, babe.

Speaking of "compliments" that land wrong . . . one time, one of my best friends, Esther, and I were sitting in a restaurant on a road trip around Washington and British Columbia. We were just minding our own business, having a girls' night, when an older white woman came over to our booth with these little cupcake stickers. She said, "I just have to say, you both are just so pretty!"

"Oh, thank you," we replied politely while exchanging a look that said, *Okay, you know something else is coming here—and it isn't gonna be good.*

We were right.

"You are both just as pretty as chocolate cupcakes," she continued. "So here are some cupcake stickers because you're both just pretty chocolate cupcakes!" She proceeded to place little cupcake stickers on both our upper chests as if we were in grade school and she was our teacher, rewarding us for giving a correct answer or something.

C: Come on . . . chocolate!? You've got to be kidding me.

A: [Sighing] No, sadly, I am *not* kidding.

And while we're on the topic of skin . . . equally ludicrous is when a white person shows off their tanned-by-the-sun-or-aerosol-can-or-light-bed skin to me and says, "I'm almost as Black as you!"

C: [Shaking his head] Sometimes I really think we just lose our minds as white people.

A: Or they take it one step further. Like when a white person has been to Africa on some kind of short-term mission trip and the Black person they are speaking to hasn't, or when they know all the words to a rap song a Black person doesn't know, or when they've read a book or seen a film considered a rite of passage for Black people, or when they do their hair in a style that is special to Black people, or when they wear "ethnic" clothing with no regard for its deep historical meaning, and then they say, "I'm Blacker than you."

C: So, apparently, not only is being Black a problem for some people, but not being Black enough is also an issue.

A: Exactly. Being Black is not some level of being that we all strive to reach, where too much or too little is a problem. Nor is it something that white people can attain by dressing or talking a certain way. Being Black is a blessing from God, Who purposefully created us, made us the way we look, and gave us the skin we're in.

It's as if there's a very specific mold that all Black people are expected to fit into, and we face criticism when we have the audacity to deviate from it by not dressing, talking, or acting a certain way or by not liking what is perceived to be "Black" food (and, yes, I'm talking about fried chicken and watermelon).

C: In other words, white people sometimes get bent out of shape when Black people don't fit the stereotype they've created.

A: Right. Not only are these stereotypes inaccurate and insensitive— they imply that everyone who is Black is the same, which could not be further from the truth! Black people are not monolithic. My Blackness may be expressed in a totally different way from the next Black person, but that doesn't make either of us less Black.

That's why I also hate it when someone asks, "What's it like to be a Black person?" as if I somehow speak for every Black person on the face of the planet. Why not just ask me about something specific, like "Adaeze, how do *you* feel about x, y, and z?" instead of trying to wrangle out a cheat sheet on how to treat all Black people?

Another example of this is when someone says, "Well, my other Black friend is okay with me saying that word or doing that thing"—the unspoken implication being, *So you should be too*. Not all Black people are the same.

Which reminds me of another microaggression: when white people constantly confuse Black people with each other. At one church where I used to lead worship, four of my friends (shoutout to Seun, Esther, Roxanne, and Keisha) would consistently get mistaken for me by white people in the congregation. They'd get a, "You did great today!" even though I was the one onstage. And this was after I'd worked there for years!

C: [Buries his face in his hands and shakes his head.]

A: I was so frustrated one day that I posted about it on social media. Two white men replied, "People get the two of us confused all the time. It's just that sometimes people get people confused." But there's no comparison between two blond-haired, dark-rimmed-glasses-wearing white men who get mistaken for each other in a sea of blond-haired, dark-rimmed-glasses-wearing white men, and four Black women of different heights, fashion styles, skin tones, and hairstyles in a church of more than three thousand people—approximately one percent of whom are Black.

C: More often than not, the people my wife is mistaken for look nothing like her. They don't have her dimples or the same face shape, skin tone, or hairstyle. I've heard people confuse Adaeze with somebody with an afro while Adaeze is in braids. It's baffling and ridiculous. Actually, it's downright insulting.

A: I think a lot of this comes down to human decency. Lumping all Black people together into one homogenous, indistinguishable group strips us of our identity. When those two white guys get mistaken for each other, they don't have to deal with the painful undertones of having been systemically unseen and faceless for more than a century.

C: This, by the way, is a great example of the blind spots we're trying to highlight—misguided ways of thinking, talking, and acting that have become so normalized that we don't even recognize how wrong they are—or why.

A: Before we move on from the "I can't believe you just said that" part of this book, there's one more microaggression I wanna point out: when white women say, "I want to marry a Black guy so I can have mixed babies."

This gets into some really disturbing territory, where Black men are degraded to the role of a "gateway" for attaining a certain look in a child. While these women may think this is a compliment, it's really a form of racism, colorism, and texturism.

C: Okay, even I'm not sure what texturism is.

A: It's a form of discrimination based on how close your natural hair is to the European—or white—standard. In other words, the coarser and kinkier your hair, the more you are perceived as less than.

C: Ouch.

A: The desire to be with someone shouldn't be based on a dream of having mixed babies, as if we're living in a video game where we can create the kinds of characters we want for ourselves or our kids. If you're a white woman and you want to be with a Black man, let it be because of the fine and wonderful man he is, not because of the skin tone you think he would pass along to your children. It's fine to admire a beautiful mixing of different races. It's another to glorify or fetishize caramel-skinned babies with curly hair and light eyes.

C: Amen to that. Adaeze and I can no longer count the number of times someone has said to us, "Oh, your kids will be gorgeous!" Yes, there is a compliment in that. Yes, there's some excitement with that. However, there's also an implication there that if our baby were either just Black or just white, it would somehow be a disappointment. That's a lot to put on a baby from the moment they arrive in the world.

YOU *DO* SEE ME, RIGHT?

A: As frustrating as it can be when white people say ignorant or hurtful things to me, what's worse is when people talk around me as though I'm not even there. For example, when Chad and I visited his grandparents in Bedford, Virginia, people there would ask Chad questions about me right in front of me instead of just asking me. They said things like, "Chad, has Adaeze met so-and-so yet?" Or "Chad, does Adaeze know about this or that restaurant here?" Or my personal favorite: "Chad, does she understand me?" said in a thick-as-syrup Southern accent. I was like, *You do see me standing here, right?*

After a while, Chad and I exchanged one of those looks that encompasses a complete conversation with no words, and I finally said, "You know, you can just ask me directly. You don't need to go through Chad."

The woman's eyes widened in surprise, and she said, "Oh! Okay!" It was as if the thought of treating me with the most basic level of respect hadn't even occurred to her.

C: Speaking of totally ignoring someone until a situation forces your hand . . . in the summer of 2020, Adaeze's phone would buzz every five minutes as one white person after another who had met her years ago but hadn't spoken to her since texted something along the lines of, "I'm so sorry. How are you? Are you okay? How's your soul?" in response to all the racial unrest unfolding on the news.

Now, I don't want to diminish this for the people of color who genuinely appreciated some of those texts, and yes, they were mostly well-intended, but think about it. If these people really cared about Adaeze, it shouldn't have taken a summer full of race riots and civil unrest to say, "Gee, I wonder how Adaeze's doing?"

A: I know most of those texts came from a good place, but what got me was all these people assuming an emotional proximity to me that did not remotely exist. For example, I received one text from someone I hadn't seen, spoken to, or texted with for three years that said, "Hey, girl! I know it's been a while, but I wanted to reach out. I'm praying for you and your family during this time. This all really breaks my heart. I'm sorry for any racism that you and your family have ever experienced. How are you doing?"

Now, as Chad said, there are probably Black people out there who had no one else reaching out to them and would have appreciated this text. I just wasn't one of them. I was busy fielding "How are you doing?" texts, emails, and calls from the people who were actually in my life, from people on social media who I didn't know personally but who felt like they knew me because they followed my accounts, *and* from people like this, who hadn't been part of my life for years but still had my number.

Granted, a lot of people in the media were actively encouraging white people to "Check on your Black friends," which is great. Of course, the key word in that suggestion is *friends*, not "the one Black person whose number happens to be in your phone." Personally, I did not have the bandwidth to explain how I was doing to everyone who asked. I was already exhausted and overwhelmed, just trying to navigate my own feelings, without taking on the additional burden of figuring out how to explain them to someone else in a way that wouldn't upset them or put them on the defense.

In fact, if I'm being totally transparent, texts like these seemed to be more about their feelings than mine. If it had really been about me, they would have considered how it might make me feel to have them suddenly reach out with such a personal question during a painful time. I'm sure a lot of them thought, *She'll feel loved and supported!* But even that proves that they didn't know me very well.

The problem is, because their intentions were noble, it's as if the way their actions came across to me didn't matter. In other words, because they meant well, I wasn't allowed to feel some type of way about it.

C: So, once again, the white person's feelings are spared at the expense of the person of color.

A: It's a tricky balance, and one Black people have to manage frequently. In the case of the white people who reached out to me even though we had no current relationship, I didn't wanna lie and just give them an answer that would make them feel better. But I wasn't gonna get into it with them either. So, for the person I mentioned earlier, I responded by saying, "Ey girl. Nice of you to reach out, thank you. Answering that question is complicated & loaded & heavy right now. I'm gonna refrain from going there in this texting convo, as I've had to take better care of myself during this time. But thank you for your care."

Of course, after sending it, I instantly wondered, *Will my thanking her and saying it was nice of her make her think she did a good thing, which she will now repeat with some other unsuspecting Black soul? Should I have encouraged her to reach out to Black people who are currently in her life?*

When her response included a repeat of "Just wanted to reach out," I lost interest in saying anything else. She had proven that her effort to reach out was about just that: reaching out. Not to make me feel loved or seen, but to check a box.

THE GOLDEN RULE

C & A: It feels a little strange to have to say this, but one of the best ways to foster healthy relationships with people of color is to—wait for it—have real relationships with people of color. Spend time with them, get to know them, ask questions—not just to satisfy your own curiosity but to genuinely learn more about them and their culture. Gather your courage and ask them to point out your blind spots if and when they see them. And when in doubt about whether something is okay to say or ask, take a breath and ask yourself how you would feel if someone asked or said something similar to you. In other words, follow the advice given in Matthew 7:12 and treat your friends of color the way you would want to be treated.

A: Speaking of which, here are the kinds of things white people say or do that make me breathe a sigh of relief because it shows they get it:

When they honor my vulnerability by being empathetic after I share about a painful racial situation.

When they listen to me and believe me when I talk about my experience of being racially marginalized without calling into question my memory, my judgment, or my ability to be a reliable narrator of my own life.

When they don't make my Black pain about their white comfort.

When they celebrate me without appropriating me—in other words, inappropriately adopting the customs or practices of my culture. This becomes especially harmful when the culture of the person doing the appropriating has a history of oppressing the other culture. For example, rap music was born out of Black struggle, but rarely is that struggle acknowledged when it's appropriated by white people. Treat my Black culture with respect, give back to and support Black culture in a way that feels right to you, and give credit where credit is due. Don't turn me or my culture into a trend or accessory.

When they resist the urge to tone-police me. As a Black woman, I'm often stereotyped as angry or hostile just for expressing my opinion. I'm told to "calm down" or to say things in a "nicer tone" when my communication isn't much different from the way my white counterparts express their feelings. Brushing me off as an "angry Black woman" or painting me as hostile, intimidating, or aggressive only allows racism and harmful stereotypes to continue. It's the easy, cowardly way out, and it dismisses what I'm communicating because I'm being incorrectly perceived as being overly emotional. When I've posted on social media about my experiences with racism, some people have brushed off my comments because I didn't say it in a way that met some white standard. It's impossible for me to anticipate how every white person would prefer me to express any sort of emotion or passion, and it's invalidating to my experiences when the focus is on *how* I am communicating, instead of *what* I'm communicating. Yes, like everyone, I need to make sure I share my message in a respectful way, but my message is not invalid just because it's accompanied by emotion. This is true especially within the church. Let's normalize the expression of emotions—these are natural human reactions! We need to accept that different people feel different emotions in different ways. If we want to engage in honest dialogue with our loved ones or coworkers of color about the racism and discrimination they experience, we must stop tone-policing.

When they uplift Black voices by being intentional about building community and creating space for me and other marginalized voices to bring our authentic selves to the table in our communities, at church, in the workplace, and in the world at large.

When they don't respond "All lives matter" to "Black lives matter." When I state that my life matters—especially in a society that has historically communicated that it doesn't—it isn't a diminishment of anyone else's life. It's just a true statement, and the fact that I feel the need to remind myself and others of that truth should be a tip-off to the pain of my experience. If someone doesn't wanna hear about that experience, fine. But when they remind me that all lives matter, it's basically like me saying, "I'm just as important as everyone else!" and then being met with "No, everyone is important." Also . . . while I do agree that tough jobs are often taken for granted, to respond to "Black Lives Matter" with a phrase like "Blue Lives Matter" puts my *life* on the same level as someone else's job. It's not the same. It communicates that my life mattering can't be true unless you throw in someone else's life mattering too. My life has historically been treated as less than. Just let me matter.

When they show respect for an ethnic name like mine instead of responding with, "Well, that's different!" They might do this by:

- Repeating my name after I introduce myself. This is reassurance, for both me and them, that they've heard my name and can say it correctly. If they need it repeated, they can just say, "I really wanna make sure I say your name correctly. Can you please teach me?"

- Double-checking the spelling of my name when writing an email.

- Teaching the pronunciation of my name to a group in advance. This can help to avoid painful or awkward encounters in a public setting.

- Kindly calling others out and correcting them if they hear my name being said wrong when I'm not present. A good tip is to jot down the pronunciation in your phone contact or in your notes app.

And when they admit that they don't get it and open the door to approach them if they get it wrong. A real-life example is a text I received from a former teammate while I was trying to address some serious issues of systemic racial sin at my workplace. She was one of the few white people I had never felt the need to talk to about this kind of stuff. Although she was out of the country while this was going down, she sent a text that was a healing balm in the midst of the frustration I was dealing with daily at work.

Honestly, I feel conviction because I've thought of reaching out for a long time—you are the closest person of color to me, and I know I have been complicit in so much systemic racial sin. I know I can't understand, but I can repent and ask that you, at least, would forgive me. I'm sorry that with all this going on that some of these efforts might seem like jumping on the bandwagon, but for me at least, the Spirit has been after me on this for a while. I'm sorry it's taken me so long, and I'm sorry for what my silence has signified. Please keep me in check if I say/behave in a way that corresponds more to my privilege than standing in solidarity.

C&A: For the record, there's no "jumping on the bandwagon" when it comes to fighting racism. Don't disqualify yourself from making an effort against racism for fear of not wanting to be weird or "too much." Racism didn't start out as a carefully thought-out plan, so we don't always need to feel like we have everything figured out before we attack it.

We've talked a lot in this chapter about blind spots—hurtful things we think, say, and do out of ignorance. It's not the worst thing in the world to be ignorant. It's what we do out of our ignorance that can either be positive or negative. We can choose to be open to learning and grow out of our ignorance, or we can stay closed off and continue to be hurtful and divisive.

The choice is ours.

CHAPTER 6

TRYING TO BE THE PERFECT BLACK PERSON

✦ ✦ ✦ ✦ ✦ ✦ ✦ ✦ ✦ ✦ ✦ ✦ ✦ ✦ ✦ ✦ ✦ ✦

A: My market salad from Chick-fil-A was hitting the spot as I sat on a couch in a small foyer at church, chomping on my lunch. The worship team and I had been working on a project all morning, and hunger had finally won out.

"Hey, Adaeze," one of my teammates called from the room behind me, "did you accidentally grab my order?"

"I don't think so," I said, my mouth still full as I rummaged through the plastic bag on the coffee table in front of me. She came over, and after failing to find her order, she wandered back into the other room to continue her search, where a few other team members were eating their lunches.

There was music playing in the room, drowning out whatever conversations were happening. I had chosen to sit separately, in part because I'd been feeling very separate from my teammates that whole summer. It was 2020, and at a recent meeting, I had finally spoken up about the racial unrest that had been dominating the news that summer. I wasn't blaming my teammates—I just wanted to be seen and heard that I was struggling. But their response, or lack thereof, showed me that my energy would be better spent elsewhere. Later on, a couple of them offered me condolences for the fact that no one had really responded to me.

It was my sixth year as the only Black person on a staff of more than 150 people, and the crappiness of 2020 had finally uncovered my tiredness. I was tired of always faking it. I was tired of repeatedly having to choose between being my most authentic self and feeling safe. I'd stopped trying so hard to be liked by and to fit in with the white people I was surrounded by all day, and I'd stopped trying to protect their feelings at the expense of my own. Though nobody said it out loud, it had been clearly communicated to me that I should "just be happy to be here," which I quickly learned meant, "Don't stir up trouble by pushing against the white status quo."

Subconsciously, I hoped that distancing myself would make it a little easier to deal with the painful reality that my white teammates and coworkers didn't care enough about me to make any changes when racial and spiritual problems within our church were brought up. So I started doing what I needed to do to feel safe. On that particular Thursday, that meant eating in another part of the room, with a literal wall dividing me from my teammates.

I wasn't in the room when it happened, but because the door was open, I heard the word loud and clear.

"Something, something, something . . . N-----!"

I froze midchew. I recognized the voice of the person who'd said it, but I couldn't make out who all had laughed afterward, though it was definitely more than one.

"What?" I said loudly in the direction of the room.

Silence.

That's it, I thought.

"Never again!" I said out loud. I hoped the strength of my comment masked how hurt, vulnerable, and unsafe I felt in that moment.

Silence.

I put the clear plastic top back on my salad and stuffed it in the bag. Tears were beginning to fill my eyes, but I was determined to fight them back until I could get out of there. I quickly grabbed my personal belongings, which I'd left on the floor just inside of the doorway. My teammate who had been looking for her lunch seemed to be the only one who saw me. She told me quietly, "I didn't say it."

Wow, want a cookie? I thought bitterly. I couldn't even look at her.

Without a word, I walked out, grabbing my lunch in stride.

I didn't see anyone on the way to my vehicle. I got in, my hands shaking as I put the key in the ignition and drove off. I didn't even know where I was going. My heart was pounding, and I was still straining to hold back the tears when I called my campus pastor. When he didn't answer, I called my boss, our senior pastor. When he didn't answer, I called Chad.

C: I was finishing up with one of my physical therapy patients when I felt the buzzing in my pocket. Adaeze knows it's difficult for me to answer my phone during the day because almost all my time is spent face-to-face with people. The fact that she was calling tipped me off that something important was happening and I needed to answer.

I shooed the person out the door just in time to pick up.

"Hey, babe!" I said lightly.

A: That's when the tears finally began to fall.

C: She wasn't even able to formulate words at first—all I could hear was her visceral sobbing. I immediately sprang into action at the clinic, moving some appointments around so I could leave right away and find Adaeze.

After about a minute, Adaeze's voice cleared up enough to speak short sentences.

A: "I think I need to be done."

C: "What do you mean?"

A: "Remember when I told you, about a month ago, I felt like I needed to leave my job before something worse happened that would *make* me leave?"

C: "Yeah . . ."

A: "It just happened."

C: The last word there hardly made it out of Adaeze's mouth before the sobs returned.

I could tell that Adaeze was in her car, driving. Fear started to well up inside me now that I realized the gravity of the situation. Adaeze was overflowing with grief, so a car didn't seem like the safest escape.

"Adaeze, where are you?"

A: "I don't know." I honestly didn't. I was so blinded by pain and frustration that once I got in my car, I just started driving. I didn't even think about where I was going. All I knew was that I wanted—no, *needed*—to get as far away from that church as possible.

C: "Okay," I said. "Pull over, drop a pin in Maps, and stay there. I'm coming."

My heart racing, I jumped in my car and sped toward her. I had visions of her curled into a ball, gasping for air through her tears.

We had made plans to drive to Glacier National Park. This was definitely *not* how I'd envisioned this weekend starting. Unbeknownst to Adaeze, I was planning to propose. In fact, I had just received the engagement ring in the mail the day before. Right now, though, all I cared about was getting to her as quickly as I possibly could.

When I found her, she was parked in an empty lot across from a McDonald's. She had made it about thirty minutes away from the church.

When I opened her door, she just clung to me.

There were no words.

We moved to the back seat so we could sit without the console between us, and Adaeze just cried. I stroked her back and sat with her. After a little while, she told me what had happened.

"I'm so sorry," I said. "What do you need?"

A: "I think I need to be done at this church."

C: I wasn't surprised to hear her say this. Honestly, if she hadn't, I probably would have said it for her. She had told me about some of her struggles at the church before, and I knew she was at the end of her rope. This moment just forced the inevitable.

"Yep," I said, "I agree."

I was scared. She didn't know I was planning to propose in a few days. Now I couldn't help but wonder how I was going to support us and what our lives would look like after she resigned. But to be honest, it didn't matter. All I knew was that I needed to protect Adaeze and be ready to do whatever the Lord was preparing us for.

A: I didn't know what I was gonna do next. I wondered if I even wanted to stay in ministry or if I should stay in Denver. For the past six years, I'd been recognized around town in association with this church, and I knew I would need a break from that, if not a complete departure. It felt like my life had officially blown up. I'd devoted so much of myself to that place, and now it was the place I most needed to remove myself from. What would happen to my relationship with Chad if I decided I needed to move? I had no idea what my future would look like now. Everything suddenly felt unfamiliar and unknown.

APPARENTLY, I'M THE PROBLEM

Hey [name of volunteer], I wanted you to hear this from me. The senior pastor accepted my resignation yesterday. I overheard someone on the worship staff say the N-word yesterday (not gonna say any names), and none of the other worship staff present said anything to defend or stick up for me. Last straw with [name of the church] for me.

A: This was the main section of the text I copied and pasted to my campus worship volunteers and a few others the day after the incident. I will never forget the subsequent phone call I got from the senior pastor, in which he yelled at me that I was trying to burn the church to the ground and accused me of not including any balancing statements. I swiftly followed up my text with this addition:

Also, I completely forgot to mention! [Name of the church] and the senior pastor are doing all they can to go about this the best way. I love and respect him to the ends of the earth. Would never mean to hurt him or [name of the church] by sharing my truth with no balancing statements!

C: I have to say, I was fuming during her phone call with the senior pastor the day after her resignation. We were on the sixteen-hour drive to Glacier, and Adaeze spent all sixteen of those hours doing damage control because, somehow, a white person using the N-word had been presented as (and had become) *her* problem.

A: Here's the thing. Being in a predominately white space usually means that Black people are expected to protect white people's feelings at all costs—even when Black people are the ones being hurt.

In this case, even though I'd voiced the truth about what happened, I did it in a way that made some of the white members of the team look and feel bad—hence the "trying to burn the church down" comment. They would have preferred me to just leave quietly without saying anything.

But I'd been in an environment where I'd felt utterly alone, rarely stood up for, and largely unseen for so long that I had reached my breaking point. My anger in the moment was used to vilify me to the rest of the church staff. Aside from a few people who reached out to tell me, "You did nothing wrong," I was seen as the one who had acted inappropriately. Even though I was neither the one who had used the N-word nor the one who laughed at it, *I* was the problem.

I was told later that when the incident was recounted in an all-staff meeting the following week, the senior pastor (who wasn't present when it happened) quoted me as having said, "Oh, no, you didn't!" in a stereotypical "Black girl" voice, casting me as the angry Black woman of the situation.

As for the guy who used the N-word? Though he was eventually let go, for weeks he was defended by the leadership and other staff members because, "You know him—he's a good guy." I never once got, "Well, we know *you*, Adaeze. You're a good gal." The fact that the phrase, "He shouldn't have said that, *but . . .*" prefaced virtually every argument in his defense while I received no such grace made it abundantly clear that, as far as they were concerned, I was the problem.

It hurt to hear messages like this, especially coming from the very community I wanted to believe was safe. I knew I wasn't alone in feeling this way either. All it takes is one false move, and what we believe to be a safe community is suddenly revealed for what it really is. If Black people aren't okay with the injustice we face and we dare to speak up about it, we are blamed. This only reinforces discriminatory and unfair standards for Black people.

In the weeks following the incident, a teammate said to me, "But, Adaeze, you know we love you." While I do believe they loved me, it became clear that their love only extended to the width of their boxes for me—boxes never designed to encompass all of me. I realized they loved me, not so much as myself, but as "the token Black person who won't upset the status quo." When I finally spoke up, it became difficult for those who said they loved me to see and love me for who I truly was. In other words, they only loved the "perfect Black person" version of me.

This is my definition of the perfect Black person. The perfect Black person shows no emotion in the moment and feels no pain. The perfect Black person has somehow thought ahead to every possible racial situation they will ever be in and has pre-fought battles so they will know exactly what to say and do in any situation so as not to offend anyone with their pain or discomfort.

Had I been the perfect Black person, I would have just laughed off the derogatory comment and said, "That's cool. It's fine." But it was not cool. And it was not fine. Had I been the perfect Black person, I would have left quietly without saying a word. But I'd been quiet long enough. Had I been the perfect Black person, I would not have gotten angry or made my white coworkers feel bad. But I was angry—not only that the incident happened, but that nobody got angry on my behalf when somebody did something that made *me* feel bad.

Sometimes overtly and sometimes between the lines, my white coworkers communicated to me how I should have reacted—how *they* would have reacted if they'd been in my shoes. But what they didn't seem to realize was that the N-word wasn't an isolated incident, as injustice rarely is. For me, this wasn't just one unfortunate comment. It was the culmination of countless microaggressions I had quietly tolerated over the course of six years in an attempt to be the perfect Black person.

I held that weight for a while, but make no mistake: it was *heavy*. The second I was no longer able to be the strong Black woman they expected me to be—when I'd finally had enough—the facade fell off, on both sides.

I CAN'T. I WON'T. I MUST.

A: Too often, Black people carry the pressure of figuring out how to act "right" based on the white people we're around. Even years after "I can't breathe," we have grown so accustomed to feeling like we need to appease the white majority that we've forgotten to respect what *we* need and what our bodies are telling us. We've forgotten to care for ourselves so we can better care for and respond to others.

I'm a believer in the Word of God, which says, "Love your neighbor as yourself" (Mark 12:31). If I'm not careful, I can feel like I have to constantly put my own feelings and needs aside for others. But the redemptive and freeing part of that verse—"as yourself"—helps me keep things in balance.

One afternoon, when Chad and I were visiting his grandparents in Virginia, we were sitting outside in a circle on the front lawn. After learning that I was a worship pastor, a friend of Chad's grandparents leaned over to me and said, "You know, our church puts on a ton of programs throughout the year, but the Black church up the road can't afford to put on programs. So our pastor goes down there to help them." Then he leaned back in his chair, a look of self-satisfied heroism on his face.

Did that old white man really just brag to me about the fact that there are still segregated churches in this town, where I'm pretty sure I would actually hear "Get out" if I tried to attend? And did he act smug about it, as if he's some white savior?

Yep.

What I wanted to say was, "So would I not be allowed in your white church because I'm Black?" But the Holy Spirit stopped me. *Don't you say that*, He gently urged me. *I don't want you to go there right now.*

As draining as it was to be the stand-in Black person on the other end of that ignorant comment, the Lord graciously reminded me that this wasn't really about me. The only way this man knew to connect with me was to talk about the segregated Black church up the road and how his church "helps" them.

Now that particular battle could have been mine if I'd chosen to step into it. But it could also pass me by without diminishing my value or my energy to fight for what I believe in. This makes it easier for me to figure out which situations and people are worth my time, breath, and energy—like the staff I worked closely with for six years—and which ones aren't, like a comparatively harmless old white man in Virginia I'll rarely see again. In other words, it becomes easier to decide which situations and which people get my "I just won't."

It's not a "can't," because Lord knows I *could*. Rather, it's a "won't" because I'll never be able to control what other people say or do around me—especially ignorant white folk. I *can*, however, control how I react.

It's a "won't" because I'm not a puppet. I've had to learn to delay my reactions at times and wait until I'm in a safe place to feel out loud. I've had to learn to not let my mood change based on how others act around and toward me or on how others want or expect me to feel. I've had to learn to take back my own body in such a way that I—not others—control if, when, and how I react.

It's a "won't" because it's not my responsibility to live up to other people's perceptions and made-up expectations of me.

I can absolve myself from burdens that aren't mine to hold. Just because racism and microaggressions happen around me doesn't mean I must fix them. Nor does it mean I must be silenced by them. It means that I get to choose if I want to use my voice against them.

Of course, "I just won't" is one sharp side of a double-edged sword. In order to survive, I constantly have to choose between that or the other sharp side of speaking up.

Sometimes loving my neighbor means not having another difficult race conversation at work, not teaching a white person about Black culture, or not entertaining a curious white person's question of, "Is all that your real hair?" Sometimes I have to remind myself that just because someone wants to engage in those conversations doesn't mean I have to. And I don't need to explain why. My boundaries are worthy of respect without an explanation. I don't have to jump just because someone else says so.

It's not that I can't. Because I definitely can. In fact, I have—and I will again. It's just that sometimes, I won't. And for me, that's perfect.

CATCHING IT FROM ALL SIDES

A: You know what's the worst? When we gotta be the perfect Black person . . . *to Black people.*

When Black people feel the pressure to be perfect from all sides, it can be beyond exhausting. Even who we fall in love with gets put under an unrealistic microscope of everyone else's opinions, standards, and expectations.

It's mind-blowing how loud a Black person can be in support of me and my art and my giftings, but as soon as they see I'm married to a white man, it's all, "You've married the oppressor." It's the "You can't say you stand for Black justice when you're married to white supremacy" idiocy.

Are we not allowed to be us and be free anywhere—even among our own race? Isn't it just another form of oppression to tell me who I can and can't love? The world continually tries to tell Black people who we should be, as if we couldn't possibly know or figure that out for ourselves.

In 2020, a few days after George Floyd's murder, a friend and I started what we called Black Hangz, a small gathering in my home where members of our community could come together to eat, mourn, heal, worship, laugh, cry, whatever— together. As it is, Black people don't have a ton of places where we can go to lay down our burdens in free and unedited ways. Gatherings like this help us lighten the load as we lean into a community of others who are feeling what we're living. Joining our voices with others going through similar experiences is empowering and uplifting, and it reminds us that we're not alone.

Yet when I posted about this on my Instagram account, I got pushback from a Black family member because we were "excluding white people." Apparently two of his extended white family members had commented that they were offended by it. So even when we as Black people try to create a safe space to process and mourn and be together, it gets put through the white strainer. The message is that if white people aren't okay with it, even celebrating our Blackness becomes "reverse racist."

How can you be the perfect Black person when even Black people don't give you their stamp of approval?

One of the most painful things about the church incident I described at the beginning of this chapter was that a well-respected Black pastor from a church in another state was called on to see if I was reacting "correctly," if I was "right about this," or if I was "overreacting." That would have been bad enough, but because his experience at his own church was so different from mine, he couldn't fully appreciate all I'd been dealing with, and he ultimately sided with the church leadership.

Though it hurt to realize that I couldn't even look to a Black person in a church leadership position for support, I also realized that just because we had the same skin tone didn't mean we'd had the same experiences. Our different experiences influenced the way we perceived the world. He simply couldn't recognize the weight of my specific situation that he wasn't in. That wasn't so much his fault as it was his reality.

There's so much more I could say about church trauma. So I did. Check out the appendix at the back of this book if this is something you're walking through too.

Once I recognized that not everyone understands or has the bandwidth for what I'm going through, it took off some of the pressure to be the perfect Black person. By the way, not getting it doesn't make these people monsters. It makes them broken and imperfect, like all of us. And once we come to grips with that, we can have more grace for ourselves and for others.

I will never be the perfect Black person. So instead of constantly preparing for the next fists-up moment, I try to focus on the present. I've done the former for years, and it's a great recipe for burning out. As for the latter, it's easier said than done. But that's okay. I'm a work in progress. We all are.

CHAPTER 7

TRYING TO BE THE PERFECT WHITE PERSON

C: It had already been a long day at work by the time I walked into the rehab all-staff lunch meeting. Since we had to cross the street from the outpatient clinic to get to the meeting, a couple of colleagues and I were a little late. We grabbed some seats along the side wall just as the first slide appeared on the screen:

DIVERSITY, EQUITY, AND INCLUSION
TRAINING

Presented by (wait for it) *some white dude.*

We began with a one-minute guided breathing exercise so we could "prepare our souls for what was about to happen."

I despise breathing exercises.

I can't slow my thoughts. Instead, my brain spins with questions like:

What am I breathing for?

What am I meditating on in this setting?

Can the person next to me hear my nose whistling from the booger lodged in my nostril?

Needless to say, I was not in the best frame of mind for what was about to happen.

In fairness, the discussion started off okay. The guy leading it talked about how in a medical facility we need to be prepared to adjust to people's needs. He talked about etiquette for using an interpreter, which was especially relevant since we were in a part of town with a large percentage of Spanish speakers. He encouraged us to learn at least basic Spanish so we could connect with patients more effectively.

He brought up attempting to understand a patient's financial situation while we're giving recommendations for their recovery. It doesn't go over well to advise someone to get a gym membership if they have difficulty buying groceries for their family.

The basic idea he was conveying was that our treatment of other people is most often a derivative of our own culture.

Makes sense, I thought.

He clicked the button, and the slide changed to: "When have you seen something that showed how important knowing culture is?"

One woman raised her hand. "We should ask how to pronounce a patient's name!"

Okay . . . kind of related to the question. Adaeze talked about the importance of names a few chapters ago. Yes, it's a great way to start honoring a person and their culture by learning to pronounce their name correctly. However, in a setting where we worked with people of all different cultures, backgrounds, and ways of life, I hoped this was a bare-minimum expectation.

Seemed like a pretty trivial example to me.

As one of the few—if not only—people in the room with a fair amount of personal experience interacting with different cultures outside work, I felt a strong pull to raise my hand and tell some stories.

I could have talked about the cultural distinctions between Adaeze's family and mine or about how patients of various cultural backgrounds tend to have different emotional responses to pain. I wanted to share my own examples of the importance of understanding another person's culture so we can understand their needs as opposed to superimposing our needs onto them.

Instead, I stayed quiet—in part because I wasn't sure my opinion would hold much weight with a group of relative strangers. They didn't know me or my story. I was just the guy who showed up late and sat on the side of the room. Plus, I had a long list of patients with challenging situations I needed to see that afternoon. I chose to save my emotional energy.

The next slide popped up: "Tell about a time when you've seen a positive or negative impact of ethnocentrism." The leader talked about the importance of trying to stay curious so we could understand each other more fully, and then he opened the floor for discussion.

Sidenote: he put the word *ethnocentrism* out there without a bit of context or explanation. I think half the room was doing a quick Google search on their phones after the word appeared. *Use common English, man. Or at least a definition would be helpful.*

One coworker talked about a time she was working with a Spanish-speaking woman who uses a wheelchair and was astonished that the patient's primary goal was to get on the floor so she could play with her kids. She enthusiastically exclaimed, "Who knew that playing on the floor with kids is so important in Mexican culture?"

My first thought was *What does that have to do with Mexican culture?* She's in a wheelchair and has children. Of course she wants to be able to get on the floor and play with her kids again!

Now I felt an even bigger pull to speak up. I wanted to tell them about the time I had a female patient who was Muslim. Her husband came with her to the appointment and stayed right by her side as we spoke. Sensing some tension, I asked a few questions to get some of her story, but she was very short and to the point. So, rather than asking more questions, I decided to address the elephant in the room.

"I just want to admit that I don't know much about your culture or your religious beliefs," I said. "So if there's anything I do during this exam that is uncomfortable for you, please let me know, and I'll be happy to adjust."

She smiled and said, "Thank you for that." With an obvious sense of relief, she continued, "My religion does not allow you to touch me."

"Okay," I said. "We can make that work."

At that moment, I saw the couple take a fresh breath. They were much more relaxed. I modified my approach slightly, and the appointment went just fine. I simply had the woman's husband do what I would have typically done while I observed. It wasn't the most thorough exam, but she felt comfortable. I was able to initiate a plan for her and get her a follow-up appointment with a female therapist so she could have better care.

But again, I decided on silence. I just didn't have it in me to speak up that day. My tank was already empty, and I wasn't even at the end of the day yet.

To my surprise, that was the extent of our diversity training for that session. I don't know what, if anything, people took from the meeting. It's not that it wasn't well-intentioned. I do applaud them for realizing that different cultures have different needs and for wanting to create awareness about that. It's just that, from my perspective, it wasn't very helpful.

For the rest of the day, I felt a restlessness in my soul telling me I should have contributed something to the discussion. When I got home, I told Adaeze what had happened.

A: After I listened to Chad tell the story (which didn't have the side commentary of him not having the energy to say anything), my first question was, "Did you say anything?"

C: "No."

A: "Why not?"

C: "I don't know. I wasn't sure anybody would actually listen. I didn't know how much good it would do, and I'm not sure how people would've reacted."

A: "Oh."

My mind was racing, trying to fill the silent and rapidly growing space between us. His biggest concern seemed to be who in the room would "get it."

I couldn't help but wonder, *If I was in that room, would I have been enough of a reason for you to speak up? Would the countless people of color you treat have been enough of a reason?*

Then a thought hit me that I didn't feel I could say aloud: *Or are we only convenient to speak up for when you aren't in a room full of white people?*

I felt ashamed for thinking that way.

Then I felt ashamed for feeling ashamed about feeling that way.

It was a learned reaction I'd been forced to pick up in order to survive being the only Black person in predominantly white spaces: protect the white person from my emotions.

The next thing I knew, I was having an argument with Chad, entirely in my own mind: *You were literally the only person in that room who could have made some actual change, and you chose passivity.*

You chose the easy way out.

You chose comfort.

You chose your white comfort.

You chose easy silence.

Because you can. Because that's your white privilege.

You'll notice how one-sided this was.

The reason I felt like I couldn't say any of this to Chad was because I didn't want him to feel like a failure—which he is not. Or feel like he couldn't do anything right. Which is also untrue.

I felt stuck. The one person I wanted to share these frustrations and feelings with was also the one whose actions had unintentionally made me feel like the scum of the earth.

C: I knew my wife well enough to know that the spiral in her head had begun. And I knew it was about me not speaking up. I was feeling very defensive, which, in turn, led to my own argument in my head.

So I just have to be perfect? I can't have an off moment?

That doesn't seem fair. I wouldn't have a problem if you did the same thing.

Apparently, my capacity doesn't matter at all.

Much like Adaeze, I was doing all the talking in my head.

We sat there in silence for a few minutes, lobbing our own private accusations. Then, because I could tell she was upset, I said, "I'm sorry I didn't speak up."

A: I knew he was apologizing only because he could tell I was upset, so I asked, "*Why* are you sorry you didn't speak up?"

C: "Because I know I carry a burden to speak up in these situations, and I knew it would hurt you if I didn't."

A: *Burden?* "So you feel *obligated* to speak up?"

C: "I do feel an obligation. For one thing, I was one of the only ones there who *could* speak into this. I also feel an obligation to you because you're part of me, and speaking up would have been defending us."

A: "Well, thank you. But you don't have to apologize."

[Awkward pause.]

"I'm gonna go use the bathroom."

C: [Awkward pause, part two.]

"Okay."

I knew we were not done with that conversation. My husband-senses were tingling. Either I was in the doghouse, or Adaeze was wrestling with emotions I didn't fully under-stand and she needed some time to herself to sort them out—aka, I was in the doghouse. So I did the natural husband thing and sat down to play *Madden* while she went to the bathroom.

A: Wait . . . when I do that, I make you feel like you might be in the doghouse?

C: Well, yeah. Whenever I say or do something that forces you to deal with your emotions, even though you may not be *telling* me I'm in the doghouse, it's kind of implied.

A: Good to know! As soon as I got upstairs, I locked both the door to our bathroom and the door to our bedroom so I could be alone. I was subconsciously hoping I could lock out my emo-tions about the situation. I had a lot to process, and I wanted space to do it without having to tiptoe around Chad's feelings.

I made a beeline for Chad's bedside table and grabbed a turquoise journal that I'd gifted him on our wedding day. Sometimes I write to him in it, as I've learned I can be most honest with him in those pages—especially when I don't feel confident enough to be totally honest with him in person.

Up until that point, most of my entries had been niceties and love letters, even the ones about some difficult situation we'd been through. This would be my first entry that was this raw and personal. I needed to get it out somewhere.

I ended up writing seven pages.

Guess I had more feelings than I thought.

C: I knew this situation was more serious than I had initially realized. Adaeze had locked herself in our room only a handful of times before, and none of them were because of something good. Worse, most of these times, if not all of them, were my fault.

The real tragedy, however, was that I really needed to use the bathroom.

I knew I needed to let Adaeze just get it all out, but I needed to get it all out too. We only had one porcelain stool, and I was locked out.

Pull it together, Chad. Get back on topic.

I was also feeling a little defensive myself. I knew I should have said something at the meeting, but I also felt like I deserved the right to stay quiet in moments when I simply didn't have the capacity to deal with it.

Unsure of what else to do, I kept playing *Madden*.

In hindsight, this may have been the wrong move.

Eventually, Adaeze opened the door, and we started getting ready for bed. We didn't talk. We just said, "I love you" and "We're on the same team."

But I had to ask, "Are we okay?"

A: I knew we needed to talk, but I didn't want to make Chad feel even worse. Besides, I had pretty much resolved not to say anything else about it, instead leaving it in the journal for Chad to read later.

In hindsight, this wasn't the healthiest thing to do—for me or for us.

Once we were in bed, lying with our backs to each other, I said softly, "It really sucks to hear that you didn't say anything. I didn't feel defended, and that hurts. But I love you. And we *are* on the same team."

C: This was the closest we'd ever come to going to bed not happy with each other.

A: Over the next couple of days, I did my best to act like everything was normal, but I was still hurt. This was unfamiliar territory for me. I don't like being upset with Chad for any reason. I'm also not the type to hold a grudge or to hold something over his head as punishment.

The longer we went without talking about it, a little voice in my head began telling me, *You don't deserve to be upset. You don't deserve to have someone speak up for you in that way anyway. You're asking too much.*

I kept going back and forth in my mind: *Was it asking too much of Chad to have him always speak up about race? Was he never allowed to sit one out if he wasn't feeling up to it?*

C: This situation reminded me of something that happened a few months into our relationship. I was driving home from work, and I called my parents for our weekly check-in. Naturally, my parents were very interested in how things were going with Adaeze. However, instead of simply checking in on a new blooming relationship, they asked questions that were mostly about the interracial piece. Granted, this was uncharted territory for them, and they had some valid questions and concerns. For some reason, though, that day the weight of constantly having to answer these questions felt particularly heavy.

I can't even remember what the conversation was about. They may have been asking if I had thought about how hard it was going to be raising mixed kids. Or maybe they were explaining the pressure they were dealing with from other family members who weren't thrilled with our relationship. Or I could have been trying to explain how Adaeze felt about the racially charged climate that characterized 2020. Regardless, I was tired.

What my parents didn't know yet was that I was already thinking about proposing to Adaeze. In the wake of this new uptick in questioning, I had a moment of revelation.

I was fighting hard for my soon-to-be fiancée.

Yes, it was emotionally taxing.

And, yes, marrying Adaeze meant that I would likely be in this fight for the rest of my life.

So . . . if I was *already* tired, what were things going to look like in five, ten, or twenty years?

For that matter, what right did I have to be tired already? Adaeze had been fighting this battle since the day she was born. And unlike me, she didn't have the option to just step out of it and sit on the sidelines when she got tired of dealing with it. I hadn't even been in this for a year. How could I be so selfish that I already wanted to throw in the towel when I had just entered the race?

My best friend needed me to be strong and fight for her. And she deserved to be fought for.

[Looking at wife in wonder.] *Honestly, babe, how do you do it?*

I understood at least some of what Adaeze was frustrated about. I also understood that I had chosen to opt out, while she does not have that luxury. And I was starting to have some sort of understanding of why Adaeze was hurt by my silence.

OKAY, NOW I'M READY

C: A few days later, we decided it was time to have a "come to Jesus" talk about this. I had a feeling Adaeze did not want to initiate it, so I did.

"I'm sorry I didn't speak up. I wanted to. I just didn't in that moment."

A: "Why not? Like, really. I want your honest answer."

C: "Honestly? Because I'd already had a long morning leading up to that meeting, including a patient who told me they'd just lost a family member and they were planning a funeral. And I knew my afternoon was going to be full of challenging patients. I wanted to say something. I had information that I thought was relevant, and I thought I could provide a perspective that wasn't being represented. I just didn't have the energy, and not saying anything felt like self-preservation."

A: That's where I was struggling. On the one hand, it's not fair for me to expect Chad to always be on, when I know I also need a break from time to time. The problem is that means I can't always count on being spoken up for. It feels like a lose-lose situation.

C: I could tell Adaeze was struggling, and I knew my next statement could either send us spiraling or bring us back together.

I began with affirmation.

"First off, I'm sorry that I made you feel like you're not allowed to be hurt. I also want you to know that my response has nothing to do with your ability to be a good wife to me. I see how this is a crappy position for you to be in. To be honest,

I let you down in that room. I want to be discerning and give my energy where I can and where it's needed, and I want to be honoring to you in speaking up when I should. Here's the hard thing for me with all of this: What do I do when I'm running on empty?"

A: I realized in that moment how much pressure Chad puts on himself—especially when it comes to being my protector. So for him to confess to me that he didn't have the capacity to speak up was pretty big. I never want him to feel that insane pressure from me.

"I appreciate all that. That is exactly what I *didn't* want you to feel—like you can't ever be running on empty or that you have to be superhuman. I sometimes feel like you have to suffer because you're married to a Black woman, and I don't like feeling that way. I don't know what the fix is. I can't change who I am and what I feel, and I love my Black woman-ness, but it's also not fair for you to feel like you can't protect your capacity. I don't want you to always feel like you're not doing enough for me or to always feel like I'm asking or expecting too much of you. In a way, it makes me feel like we are proving all the people right who are against interracial marriage, and I hate that."

C: "I don't ever want you to feel that you are asking too much of me. And I don't ever want you to feel that you aren't important enough for me to speak up for. But we're definitely not proving the doubters right. The fact that we can have conversations like this is proof that we'll be okay. The fact that we missed each other is just a testament to the reality that we're married, and this stuff happens."

Let's zoom out a little bit for a second. We've been talk-ing about these concepts as they relate to marriage because Adaeze and I happen to be married, but the concepts apply on a broader scale too. Adaeze and I got into a little bit of an argu-ment there, but that isn't necessarily a bad thing—in a marriage or in a friendship.

The closer we draw toward others, the more opportunity we have to see things differently. That friend, that colleague, that neighbor—each of them has a story that will challenge our view of the world. You may even enter a disagreement when your backgrounds bump against each other. That is the time to lean in!

It's like Jacob wrestling with God (Genesis 32:22-31). Jacob may have walked away with a bad hip and some scars, but he dug in and stayed in the fight. It was after this event that God changed Jacob's name to Israel, forever altering the trajectory of the people of God. The blessing came after the wrestling.

I'm not saying you should force a conversation with some-one who is unwilling to dive in with you, but there is some-thing special—almost sacred—about honestly struggling with someone to find common ground. Adaeze and I have made the most significant strides in our relationship during these wres-tling moments because they force us to go to deeper places than we'd go otherwise. We come out on the other side with more understanding, more love, and more respect for each other. As a white man, I know my skin color is the living embodiment of a huge part of her pain. Her willingness to engage with that is precious and deserves respect.

A: Likewise, Chad's humility in understanding what his skin color represents in these situations and his willingness to engage with me while treading intentionally also deserves respect.

C: In that moment, Adaeze needed me to come to her with humility and honesty, and she needed to be able to share her feelings without fear of judgment. For my part, I needed to be willing to accept that I could be wrong. I also had to accept that—despite all my perfectly valid reasons for not speaking up—there was still pain in that for her. Adaeze needed me to hear that, not just because I am her husband but because we're best friends.

All close interracial relationships will eventually hit deep, choppy waters like this. When they do, we need to be honest and allow honesty from the other side. And in order to fully understand, we need to be able to listen without taking personal offense.

A: I realized I needed to be better about making space for Chad's capacity and be willing to acknowledge that some of these conversations can be just as emotionally draining for him as they are for me. I need to recognize that one instance of him staying silent does not negate all the other times he *has* spoken up for me.

C: Thank you. And I always want you to be free to say what you need to say. I realize that sometimes it's not easy, but I really do want to support you and be with you. So please tell me what you're thinking. I may not always understand or even get it right, but I'll never stop trying.

A: Deal.

HAVE A LITTLE GRACE

C & A: Because of our histories, we have different capacities when it comes to dealing with racial issues and conversations. Where Chad's capacity is like an oil lamp that occasionally runs out and needs to be refilled, Adaeze's capacity is more along the lines of a totally burned-out wick. And you know what? Both are valid and okay.

In the same way that we have different capacities when it comes to dealing with the race conversation in general, we also have different capacities when it comes to how we respond to the race conversation at any given moment.

A: I used to have way more capacity to fight and teach others, but I've learned that I can't be responsible for teaching everybody. Frankly, I've become a bit exhausted from the pressure of feeling like it was always expected of me. Sometimes all I can do is hope and trust that someone else will have enough capacity to make up for what I might lack on any given day.

C: I have not faced the same expectation to teach others that Adaeze has, and while I may not be as exhausted from the constant engagement with it as my wife is, on any given day I might be too emotionally spent from dealing with other things to willingly jump into a conversation about race.

A: Just like I would want others to give me grace when they expect me to be the voice of reason/truth/empowerment and all the other things, and just like I desire understanding when my capacity is too low to engage with it all, I want to have grace for Chad when he is caught in a similar situation. Just because we don't share the same history doesn't negate his feelings or make them less important. Both can—and do—exist.

C: Ultimately, being the perfect white person really comes down to having the humility to understand the sheer impossibility of that achievement. We simply are not "all that and a bag of chips," and no matter how hard we try, we never will be because there's a limit to what we can truly understand. Not to mention that, as human beings, we are also inherently fragile and self-centered. We are quick-tempered. We can be manipulative. We like to stay where we feel comfortable. Simply put, we are all broken people, and that's okay as long as we're willing to admit it. If we march into the storm with an understanding that we're flawed, it's much easier to have grace for others.

My encouragement for anyone wanting to be the best, most supportive white spouse, friend, or coworker you can be is this: stay real, listen fiercely, stay vulnerable, and have patience. The more you keep your walls down, the fewer walls will go up in front of you. And be gracious when the other person isn't ready to talk. Remember, it's not your story to hear—it is theirs to tell.

C & A: This is why we need to follow Jesus' lead, to really lean in and see the depths of one another, like He did. In Jesus' day, the cultural norm between Jews and Samaritans was hostility or, at the very least, avoidance. The Jews considered themselves superior to the Samaritans because, while the Jews were the direct descendants of Abraham, the Samaritans were a mixed race that resulted when Jews from the north intermarried with Gentiles from other regions (yes, this kind of racial nonsense has been going on *that* long!).

The two groups hated each other so much that when Jews were traveling, they would go miles and sometimes even days out of their way to walk around Samaria, just to avoid running into a Samaritan. Of course, Jesus, being completely without prejudice, had no qualms about visiting a Samaritan village. But when the Samaritans were, shall we say, less than hospitable toward Jesus and his followers, James and John asked Jesus to "call down fire from heaven to burn [the Samaritans] up" (Luke 9:54). Needless to say, Jesus was not having it, and he put James and John in their place.

Later Jesus shared a parable with His disciples about a Jew who was traveling alone when he was attacked and robbed by bandits. They beat him up, took his clothes, and left him on the side of the road to die. Both a priest and a temple assistant came along and saw the man, but instead of helping him, they passed him by. Then a Samaritan approached. He not only tended the man's wounds but put the man on his donkey, brought him to an inn, and took care of him the entire evening. The next morning, he gave the innkeeper two silver coins and said, "Take care of this man. If his bill runs higher than this, I'll pay you the next time I'm here" (Luke 10:35, NLT). The Samaritan didn't look at the man on the side of the road and see someone "different" to be despised or avoided. He just saw a fellow human being who was in need of care and compassion.

That's what Jesus calls us to do: take care of one another and love one another—even if the person in question is not one of our "own people." Nobody made in God's image should be left in their dirt alone.

So when the going gets tough and we're not sure what to say, what to do, or how to respond, that's not the time to shut down or run away. That's when we need to hold on tight and fight even harder for each other. We might not always get it right, but we can't stop trying.

CHAPTER 8

GETTING ON THE SAME TEAM

A: The hot water of the shower ran over my body, drowning out the sound of my sniffles. From the pit of my stomach, a resigned pressure rumbled up to my chest. As much as I tried to practice positive self-talk, scenes of me jogging down a street like Ahmaud Arbery, being chased by men in a truck, kept running through my mind.

We were fresh out of 2020 and all the racial unrest that year had wrought—far too many stories about innocent Black men and women being hunted down in Georgia (Ahmaud Arbery), murdered while sleeping in Kentucky (Breonna Taylor), and casually choked on the street in Minnesota (George Floyd). It still felt very fresh for me. I was being careful about where I went and who I was around socially, and it was not helping to imagine having to slink down in the passenger seat of our rental car as Chad and I drove through the streets of Bedford, a town not far from Lynchburg, Virginia.

I wanted so much to do what my husband was asking of me, yet this was the moment my first panic attack decided to invade my life. My body was reacting to something I hadn't yet experienced firsthand, although I'd lived traces of it and similarities to it. Despite the constant triggers reminding me what I was up against, I wasn't aware of how continual my self-care needed to be.

My body was holding so much tension—not only from the painful (and racially-charged) exit from my previous job months earlier but also from the job I had just started, where I was once again the only Black person on staff, and from all the racial tension in the world at large. As much as my head wanted to believe *You're okay! It's gonna be great!* my body was already in protection mode.

I kept trying to talk myself down.

You are fine.

You are strong.

You are going to be okay.

Nothing was working.

I felt suffocated by the hot, steamy air in the shower. In an attempt to catch my breath, I doubled over. I tried to validate my feelings while at the same time telling myself I was over-reacting. I don't think I had ever felt more alone, which only escalated the feelings of panic.

It was like all the experiences where I felt different in predominantly white spaces were coming to a head, and anything I said to Chad would only confirm what I feared most: that I *was* weak. Yet I felt like saying yes to what was being asked of me might result in my becoming the next victim of a hate crime hashtag.

C: Up until this point, Adaeze and I had only communicated with my grandparents via Facetime or over the phone. But after six months of marriage, we were at the point where my parents were encouraging us to visit them in Virginia. We hadn't made the trip yet, partly because by the time we were far enough into our relationship to have a "meet the family" experience, COVID-19 had shut down travel. Even our wedding happened during lockdown.

The other reason we hadn't made the trek to Virginia was because the town my grandparents lived in bore a striking resemblance to the diner we'd visited in the mountains of North Carolina. My grandparents were also the ones who'd had the most difficulty accepting our relationship. Given all of this, we had decided it was best for us to not put ourselves in that situation. But now my parents felt it was time to rip off the Band-Aid.

In my mind, the phone call with my parents went well, with Adaeze and me closing with a noncommittal, "We'll talk about it."

As soon as we hung up, I said, "So are we going to Virginia?"

A: "Where are *you* at with it?"

C: "Honestly, I think we should go. I don't know if there's going to be an easier time to do it. Yeah, it's going to be uncomfortable, but I think we kind of need to just do it."

A: "Why? Like, why do we *need* to just do it?"

C: "Well . . . my parents are going to keep asking. If we just get it over with, it'll take the pressure off."

A: "It just feels like no one is taking into account what this will be like for me."

C: "Well . . . can we come up with a compromise?"

A: "I don't know. I feel like I'll have to be the one to concede."

C: "What if we fly into a bigger city, go to my grandparents' place during the day, and stay at a hotel in the city at night?"

A: "Hmm . . . maybe."

C: I was very aware that it was going to be an uncomfortable trip for both of us, but I thought we had figured out a way to do it and still make Adaeze feel safe. I was operating from the understanding that we'd agreed to go, but that night, while I was downstairs folding laundry, Adaeze was upstairs in the shower breaking down.

I was completely oblivious to how Adaeze was feeling until I went upstairs and heard quiet sobbing coming from behind the shower curtain. That was the moment I realized we had completely missed each other. Now the pressure was crushing my best friend, and I felt terrible that I hadn't noticed it earlier.

We talked, but Adaeze didn't say much. One thing was clear, though. We could not go to Virginia right then.

I went back to my parents and told them that we were gonna have to pass. I made up some excuse, and they responded well, but they were still adamant that a meeting between my grandparents, Adaeze, and me take place.

ONE SMALL STEP

C: The following summer, my parents invited my grandparents out to their house in Spokane for a big family gathering. This was a much better option for us.

A: Meeting Chad's grandparents for the first time in Spokane felt a lot safer to me because I had been there once before with Chad to visit his family. It felt more known, and this trip would be with other people in Chad's family we got along well with. So, yes, this was *definitely* a better option.

C: Because there would be a lot of people at my parents' house for this gathering, they were planning to have us sleep in the open basement. As gracious as that was, I had to talk to them about how important it would be for us to actually have a bedroom. I explained to them how difficult this situation would be—for Adaeze specifically and for both of us. Even though this was a more familiar place, we knew there was a good chance we'd be facing some racially-charged situations over the next couple of days, and we needed a place to go behind closed doors and let down our guard a little bit.

My parents understood, and they got us into a bedroom, but the fact that I had to voice this concern was part of the reason I knew this was going to be a stressful weekend. We were stepping into a situation where we would have to fight for our peace.

This is not meant to be a knock on my parents—they went out of their way to put this gathering together, and they wanted to make it as successful as possible. We were in a phase of learning a new normal, where I was no longer the lone single person in the family. My family was learning how to treat me as a married man as well as how to welcome Adaeze as my wife. We had to make it known what we'd need to make this trip as successful as possible.

A: I thought we were put in that room from the start. I didn't even know you'd had that conversation with them until just now. Thank you.

C: You're welcome!

When we got to Spokane, everything went about as expected. My grandparents were there. They were kind. Adaeze hugged them, and they said something along the lines of, "We're happy to finally meet you." Things got off to a pretty good start.

A: From everything I'd heard about Chad's grandfather, I was braced for certain comments to come out. Some of those comments *did* come out, but they were directed more toward women in general, revealing his outdated understanding of women's abilities through subtle jabs thrown out as jokes. After a little while, I started to relax a bit more around him—so much so that one afternoon, I sat with him on the balcony. Other people trickled into the house, and eventually it was just him and me. And it was okay. He rambled about the farm he and Chad's grandmother lived on, which he was very proud of. He asked me zero questions to get to know me, but I wasn't expecting any.

C: Adaeze didn't know that I was watching like a hawk from the kitchen. I was acquiring a Superman cape of sweat down my back as I watched their interaction unfold, but everything seemed okay. I didn't see any signs of stress or discomfort from my wife. She was facing my grandpa the entire time and seemed to be genuinely engaging with him. Sure enough, when Adaeze came back inside, she was fine. She actually seemed happy about the conversation. It was a beautiful thing to watch God begin the process of bringing peace to this storm.

A: It was a win, for sure. It might have seemed small to everyone else, but it was pretty big for me. I definitely felt God's peace cover me as I sat there with someone I wasn't expected to get along with. I knew it wasn't proof that Chad's grandfather was a changed man. However, it was nice that we could just sit on a balcony and chat for twenty minutes or so and have everything be okay. In fact, in the two days Chad and I were there, nothing major happened. When we left, I let out a sigh of relief, but there was also a feeling of accomplishment—not just with Chad's grandparents but with his family in general.

C: It did feel like a huge victory. I was grateful (and honestly, a little surprised) that we were able to meet my grandparents face-to-face and have nothing disastrous happen. And the fact that Adaeze was able to let her guard down a little and give more of herself to my family was so healing. There were still some misunderstandings that needed to be worked through, and we knew we would still have battles to overcome in the future, but this was a step in the right direction.

FOR BETTER OR WORSE

A: The next opportunity we had to be around Chad's grandparents came over a year later. We were attending the wedding of Chad's cousin to his longtime girlfriend.

C: The wedding was in the relatively diverse city of Virginia Beach, so it was still a somewhat inviting area for us. We got to see a slightly different side of my family this time though. Now that we were past the first meeting, people were no longer on their best behavior. There were a few moments when someone was a little loose with their tongue and made a comment that was mostly benign but still questionable, and a few actions that Adaeze and I had to process after the fact to discern the person's intent. Nothing terrible happened or was said, but Adaeze and

I had to spend a lot more time figuring out what to bring up, what to swallow, and how to be the best teammates we could for each other.

A: On the night of the rehearsal dinner, there was a dinner for just family and close friends of the couple. At one point, Chad and I decided to take a restroom break together. (No, not like *that*.) Being the gentleman he is, Chad had me walk in front of him. The story that follows is part of why I usually prefer to walk behind him.

On the way out, I had to walk through a group of Chad's family members, and it wasn't until I reached the building where the restrooms were that I realized my husband was no longer behind me. As I turned around to look for him, I saw he had been cornered and separated from me. I immediately felt a wave of exclusion, as if Chad's family had deliberately waited for me to pass by so they could talk to him alone. And because I'd just walked by, it felt less like I hadn't been seen and more like I wasn't wanted. Or possibly a little bit of both.

Stop it, Adaeze, I silently scolded myself, my armor of toughness beginning to form. *Don't play the victim.*

Still, I couldn't help but feel as though my teammate had left me out there in the dust instead of calling me to join him once we were separated. As I turned to walk—alone—into the building, I silently wished Chad would ask me to join him to show his family that we were one, together—even if that was less comfortable for them to digest.

I hid out in the restroom for a little bit, gathering myself with a pep talk and reminders that, even though I was the only Black person at this event, I wasn't alone.

But I feel very alone.

I looked at my reflection in the mirror. "You are a strong Black woman," I told myself. "And you don't need people to include you to know your worth."

Drawing some confidence from the movie *The Woman King*, which we'd seen the previous month, I added an encouraging "Agojie!" for good measure and finally left the restroom. Walking back out into the dark, I hung out at the outdoor snack table, lingering there for a while in an attempt to not make things more uncomfortable when I walked back into the dining room. How that would have made it less uncomfortable, I don't know, but that was my plan.

C: My family had stopped me to ask me to hang out on the "adult side" of the table when we came back.

Yes, we are in our thirties and we weren't on the adult side of the table. Granted, everyone else on our side of the table was also in their thirties, so I guess it was more of a "young adult side" and an "over the hill" side. Regardless, by the time I got outside, Adaeze was already gone. When I went back to the dining room, I expected to find Adaeze in her chair, but she wasn't, so I sat down to wait for her. When she didn't come back, I went outside to look for her and found her next to the snack table.

I wasn't surprised. (By the way, if you're ever looking for my wife, find the snack table. She's probably next to it.)

I could tell she was shaken up. She told me about feeling left out when my family opened the gate for her to go through and then shut the gate on me. It made sense. I could see how alienating it was for her and how easy it would have been for me to call her back so she would feel more a part of things.

A: The thing we learned about each other on that trip was not so much how to react to other people's actions but how to be a team no matter what other people do to or around us. Sure, it hurt that Chad didn't call for me when we were separated. But what hurt most about the gate-opening situation was that Chad went back in without me afterward, without waiting for me.

I didn't expect that kind of consideration or understanding from Chad's family, but given all the conversations we'd had about being a team leading up to this event, I *was* hoping for a different response from Chad. I wanted to know he was with me, no matter what other people said or did—subconsciously or purposefully—to make it appear that we weren't.

C: Up to this point, I had been a decent mediator of my family to my wife, but I hadn't really figured out how to be a good mediator of my wife back to my family. Without realizing it, I had been writing these things off as, "I'm just the one they're comfortable with because I've known them my whole life." I hadn't taken the extra weight of the racial dynamic into account because, when things like this happen, the question *Is this because I'm Black?* will always pop into Adaeze's head. Whether it is or not, as her husband and teammate, I need her to not feel alone in that.

At the end of that trip, I actually felt better than after we went to Spokane. Not because it was easier—it was the more difficult trip. But I felt like Adaeze and I had picked up some valuable tools to help us come together more effectively as a team.

The best part of the trip, though, was on our flight back to Denver. Adaeze looked at me and said, "I think it's time to make the trip to go see your grandparents in Bedford."

I could not have been more proud of my wife than when she said that. It reflected all the work she'd been putting in with my family. It also made me proud of my family. It was proof that they had also come a long way and had made Adaeze comfortable enough to be willing to do the very thing that a few months prior had triggered a debilitating panic attack.

THIRD TIME'S THE CHARM

C: That summer, my whole family decided to go to Bedford. My grandmother had not been doing well healthwise, so the idea was to get everyone together one last time at the family farm.

A: Like with the trip to Spokane, the fact that we wouldn't be the only ones going helped me feel more comfortable with the idea. What I didn't realize until the day we were leaving for Bedford, however, was that we would be staying in Chad's grandparents' home—just a tiny detail that got missed because Chad was used to that arrangement any time his family went to visit.

I also learned that our brother-in-law wasn't gonna be there. He was one of the only people in the family we were confident would stand up to Chad's grandfather with Chad if anything was said that wasn't okay. Neither of these revelations helped my comfort level, but I still felt all right about going.

But once we got there, I sensed something about the atmosphere that set me on edge.

C: It really was reminiscent of that diner in North Carolina. There was a palpable shift in the atmosphere when we got off the airplane. It's difficult to convey in tangible terms what created this shift. Some of it was looks we got; some of it was people's tone of voice when addressing us. But there was a difference that was as clear as the humidity drenching my already sweating skin. The whole time we were there, Adaeze and I were on edge. There was no place to take a breath, nowhere for us to just relax.

The entire trip was riddled with cultural blinders and unaware comments. Some of my grandparents' guests came over and spoke to Adaeze in ignorant ways. This is when a neighbor who was being introduced to Adaeze skipped eye contact with her, went straight to me, and asked, "Can she understand me?" Overall, there was a consistent feeling of Adaeze being treated like a second-class citizen. It felt like we were wearing a weighted vest from the time we got there until we left. I don't think Adaeze was really able to decompress until we landed in Denver. It took a long while for the effects of that environment to wear off.

A: That's not to negate the fact that I had some really good moments with Chad's grandfather on the trip. A couple of times, I got to talk to him—just me and him—usually in a group of people but just off to the side. God continued to give me those little moments without me looking for them.

One of the most special moments came after Chad's grandmother suffered a health issue while we were there. I noticed Chad's grandfather had tears in his eyes, so I told Chad, "I'm gonna go check on him."

I walked over to Chad's grandfather, put my hand on his shoulder, and simply asked, "How are you doing?"

Immediately, his hand rose to his shoulder and grabbed my hand. He started talking to me, and eventually I grabbed my leftover Oreo milkshake from Cook Out (a place I did not know of before this trip, but thank you, Bedford, for teaching me about it), pulled up a chair next to him, and listened to this man who needed a compassionate ear. He shared his version of how things had been with Chad's grandmother's health, and I listened, nodding and "mm-hmming," for about fifteen minutes.

After we got home, I got a sweet text from one of Chad's family members, thanking me for the way I loved on their grandfather while we were there. In the text, she said she didn't know how much it took for me to sit down next to him and show him that kind of love and compassion, and she thanked me for being willing to come and for showing their family "a whole lot of grace." That alone was confirmation that this was bigger than us, bigger than me. We also got to bring home some spotted calla lilies from Chad's grandmother's yard, which felt like a tangible reminder of the beautiful, redemptive work God was doing in these relationships.

C: Challenges aside, I am so grateful that we went. Not only was it the most meaningful encounter my grandparents have had with Adaeze, but Adaeze and I grew closer through the experience. She had the opportunity to learn more about me and my origin story, which helps her understand in a broader context where I'm coming from. I was able to be a more effective teammate to her during a really stressful situation, and I got to see more of the warrior in my wife. I also got a sense of how deeply my wife loves me, as evidenced by her willingness to subject herself to something she knew would be incredibly difficult for her.

C & A: Even though this trip was emotionally straining from start to finish, there was also so much beauty to behold. Holding that dichotomy of pain and progress simultaneously is okay—and sometimes we need to do just that. Those three trips, and especially the last one, show the power of presence.

C: Did we get everything right? Absolutely not. And to clarify, by *we*, I mean my white family here. We absolutely did not get everything right.

Did Adaeze and I get everything right? Nope. We tried, though, and our relationship is better because of it.

Relationships between people who are different from one another do not come without hardships. They don't come without difficult moments. My parents and grandparents are not always going to do the perfect thing, nor will Adaeze and I. But the more we're around each other with hearts postured toward humility and love, the more we will grow.

C & A: We're still not journeying to where we need to be. There's not always a weightlessness of being all that we are at all times. Growth is happening, though. Reconciliation is happening, even if it's a slow process. A genuine relationship isn't achieved in a lightning-rod moment, and then everything's all good. It's a beautiful journey—one that we're all slowly and steadily walking together.

CHAPTER 9

PLEASE STOP SAYING, "I DON'T SEE COLOR"

A: At some point, either during our engagement or shortly after we were married, we had a long talk with Chad's parents about our differences—not just mine and Chad's, and not just about our skin color, but about my family and their family and the different ways we think, communicate, respond, and react to things. Chad's dad—with his kind heart and with complete genuineness—said to me, "Adaeze, we don't see you as any different. We see you as our daughter-in-law and part of the family."

While the last half of that sentence was beautiful, I had to gently explain to him that the first part didn't make me feel seen at all because it implied that all my experiences that have been totally different from his were being consciously or sub-consciously pushed aside for the sake of some false sense of sameness and uniformity. The heart behind it was great, but it wasn't an accurate reflection of the vast differences in our realities.

I told him, "I want to be accepted as part of the family and as your-all's daughter-in-law *with* all of the differences we have, not *in spite of* them."

C: Not long ago, I had a conversation with a college student over coffee, and he told me about a time he was in a traveling church choir. He had an epiphany during one of the services. "I looked out and everybody just looked the same to me. I thought, *This is how I should always see people around me. I shouldn't be worried about what people look like.*"

But the truth is my and Adaeze's different skin colors *do* change how the world sees and interacts with us. When we claim not to see color, all we are doing is superimposing ourselves onto someone else. The reality we have to wrestle with is that people of different ethnicities have different experiences that we do not understand.

A: The language of "I see everyone the same" or "I don't see you as any different," when we clearly are, may be well-intended. However, unless you acknowledge and accept my differences, you will never fully appreciate how or why my experiences are different from yours.

C: And you will never get to know the full beauty of God's creation, which is a multiethnic, multicultural, and deeply diverse conglomerate of experiences, backgrounds, and beliefs—all of which are unified under Christ. His awesome sovereign design is far beyond our understanding, yet the more we lean in and embrace one another's differences, the more we see the depth and width and breadth of His love for His creation.

A: Let's face it: there is no "normal." We are *all* different. We all grew up in different environments, with different lenses we use to see the world and with different ways of communicating and expressing ourselves. Take the conversation Chad and I had on our way back from a hiking trip a few years ago . . .

HOW CAN YOU NOT SEE THIS?

C: Midway through the summer of 2020, after we'd been dating almost a year, Adaeze and I drove to the mountains to go hiking. It was a beautiful day with bright blue skies—not too hot, not too cold. Butterflies were still swirling around us, both literally and figuratively. We had just started dating, so we were still acting all flirty and trying to put our best foot forward. It was great.

As we were driving home, we started talking about the recent murder of George Floyd. I was very much in the dark about how something like this might be hitting Adaeze, and even though I had no understanding of the communal pain the Black community was feeling at the time, I wanted to talk about how I could help her as she processed everything.

A: The more we talked, the more my emotions began to rise, and my voice became more animated. I had a lot of pent-up emotion surrounding George's murder, and when Chad asked me about it, the dam just broke open.

C: This conversation didn't go quite as I expected. Adaeze got emotional and broke down in tears, frustrated not so much by the conversation itself but by the harsh reality of the world she, as a woman of color, lived in.

I felt totally out of my depth and honestly had no clue what to do. So I put my hand on Adaeze's leg and just kind of gripped it. Then, in an attempt to comfort her, I said something to the effect of, "You're okay—we're just talking about this." That's when Adaeze completely shut down.

A: It felt like he was silencing me. It was one of the first times in our relationship that I wondered if my emotions and the things I had to go through as a Black woman would be too much for Chad.

I physically turned away from him—I thought subtly—and looked out the window, feeling like I needed to hide the tears that were sneaking down my face. I suddenly felt like I was "too much" for my white boyfriend.

C: She wasn't hiding her frustration very well. I paused for a beat or two, and then I cautiously asked, "Hey, what happened there? Why have you been looking out the window for the past few minutes?"

A: "Because it felt like you were trying to silence me and shut me down."

C: "Oh, that was not my intention at all. I was just trying to let you know that it's okay, and I'm here."

A: "Yes, but the way you did it made me feel like I was too much for you or like you needed to 'calm me down,' when I was just telling you how I feel."

C: "It just felt like you were starting to work yourself up. I was trying to bring you back here—to remind you that it's just you and me talking about this right now."

A: "And I'm trying to tell you I'm not 'getting myself worked up.' What we're discussing is very upsetting. And even though it's just me and you talking right now, this is still my very real reality, and it can be painful. When I talk about it, I'm going to feel that pain."

C: "That's totally fair. I just didn't realize this conversation was going to stir up this kind of emotion for you. If you'd rather not talk about it right now, we don't have to."

A: "Well, I *wanted* to, but then you shut me down. And, babe, you're not always going to be able to anticipate what my reaction will be, because we don't live in the same reality. If you really want to help me feel more comfortable talking to you about it, please just let me feel it, and sit in it with me."

C: What Adaeze was saying made complete sense to me. I just wasn't used to that level of emotion during conversations. It's not the way my family communicated when I was growing up. I'm used to the classic dad who doesn't want to cry, so he'll stop talking for a while until he's more composed, even if it takes him like twenty freaking minutes to get through two sentences.

A: Whereas in my family, we talked most things out. Suppressing emotion wasn't really a thing I learned how to do—with one exception. I was told, "Don't cry," a lot. I was always told that I had to be strong. So I guess I did have to suppress my emotions somewhat. But I didn't want to have to do that with Chad.

C & A: Both of us came into the relationship with certain learned behaviors and expectations based on how we were raised and the kinds of things we heard growing up. As a result, sometimes when one of us says one thing, the other hears something else. We call them family filters. We all have them. They color the way we see, hear, think about, and react to things. And, man, can they cause a lot of conflict.

A: One night, our friends Orin and Amaris (aka "Oris"!), who are also an interracial couple, had us over to their place for a double date over a dinner of salmon tacos (they get me). As we went to town on the tacos, they told us about two questions they ask when they feel like they're missing each other: "What am I hearing because of my family filter? What are you hearing because of your family filter?"

Because of Chad's family filter, my emotions in the car felt inappropriate, shocking, and unfamiliar. It made him think that something was wrong, needed his fixing, and that he needed to calm me down to correct and change what I was feeling.

C: In my family, that kind of emotion was not typical. My parents never fought in front of people, especially us kids. So I learned to do the same: retreat to control my emotions and then speak. I tried to comfort Adaeze because I felt like the conversation was no longer productive with her heightened emotions.

A: I grew up in an environment where talking about things with each other was a sign of respect, love, and trust. However, because I also grew up with the family filter of strength, meaning not crying, Chad's attempt to stop me from crying made me feel like I was back in the environment of needing to buck up, be "strong," and not cause a scene or make anyone feel uncomfortable.

C: In my family, any emotions other than joy were supposed to be suppressed in conversation. When we let our emotions fly, it was treated as a sign of weakness or lack of control. When Adaeze got emotional over a question I asked, it made me feel like I had crossed a boundary that I shouldn't have crossed.

I was trying to console her, but to her, it felt like I was no longer safe. And when she pulled away, I felt like I was being rejected.

A: Having grown up in a family where I was unintentionally taught the opposite, it was huge for me to trust somebody to the point where I'm not only showing my emotions but fully feeling them while continuing the conversation. Because—surprise, surprise—women can cry *and* carry on an intellectual conversation at the same time, cuz we're awesome, we're bawsses, and we don't need to suppress our emotions in order to think straight and continue talking to you level-headedly.

C: Sidenote here: men, we can do the same thing.

A: EYOOO!

As a Black woman in a world that tells me I'm not allowed to be anything but *A STRONG BLACK WOMAN*, it has taken me a long time to come to terms with my beautiful emotions, to accept that it's okay to feel those emotions without being controlled by them, and to realize that doing so does not make me "too emotional" or "too sensitive." So it wasn't just that Chad reacted the way he did. There was a lot of negative history he unknowingly repeated for me in a moment when I was already feeling intense pain.

C: We were actually seeking the same common ground. We were just coming at it from opposite directions because of the way we'd learned to express ourselves. Since I didn't know about Adaeze's family history or fully understand the cultural pressure she was operating out of, I responded in a way that was neither helpful nor fair to her.

I WAS COLORBLIND, BUT NOW I SEE

A: Because we are two different people representing two different cultures who live in two different realities, we've had to learn how to communicate with each other and how to sit with each other while fully appreciating the other person *and* our differences. It takes a lot of time and patience, and this isn't possible if we just see each other as extensions of ourselves. We have to see our differences in order to truly respect and appreciate someone else.

C: My beautiful wife is one hundred percent correct. If we don't take the time to see everything that has come behind a person, there's no way we will be able to truly see the person who's sitting right in front of us.

A: Why do we accept the idea that we have to ignore the differences in our lovely skin tones in order to live peaceably with each other? Let's upend the phrase "I don't see color." Even if it's only intended figuratively, it doesn't need to be said. For one thing, unless we're talking about actual colorblindness, we do see different skin tones. It's a shame some people feel a need to ignore or overlook something we should all love about ourselves—our skin. Second, contrary to the unspoken popular opinion, this statement doesn't make people of a different race feel seen. In fact, it has the opposite effect. People of color are already seen as minorities—we don't need more help in not being seen. Please, see us and everything that makes us *us*—and don't apologize for seeing it. Celebrate it! Let's have conversations about it.

C & A: Being "colorblind" and ignoring our differences isn't the answer. The answer is treating people who look different from you with respect.

Because of all the racial crap that has gone on in the world, some people feel nervous being around a person of a different race—not because they're racist but because they don't want to offend anyone. In fact, they may want to show support for the person—especially in the wake of racially charged incidents in our country—but they don't know how.

That pressure is understandable, but it's time to take that extra pressure off ourselves and treat everyone with respect, regardless of skin color. If you're not sure how to do this, that's okay. It's a journey; just keep listening, loving, and putting in the time until you do.

This makes us think about Paul's classic love verses: "Love bears all things, believes all things, hopes all things, endures all things" (1 Corinthians 13:7, ESV). We miss that when we "don't see color," because we're all different. That's the way God made us, and it's beautiful. When we choose to love only those who look and sound exactly like us, it doesn't do justice to the love the Lord showed us in the first place (Romans 5:8; Matthew 5:43-48). So, if we are truly going to love people and show the love of Christ through our actions, we have to love people for who they are—and that means seeing all the beautiful things that make them different from us.

In fact, let's make this even easier, because, at the end of the day, it all boils down to one command. Jesus said, "A new commandment I give to you, that you love one another: just as I have loved you, you also are to love one another. By this all people will know that you are My disciples, if you have love for one another" (John 13:34-35, ESV).

That's it. Love. Everybody. For exactly who they are.

Got it?

Cool?

Good talk.

CHAPTER 10

CELEBRATING WHAT WE DON'T UNDERSTAND

◊ ◊ ◊ ◊ ◊ ◊ ◊ ◊ ◊ ◊ ◊ ◊ ◊ ◊ ◊

C: When we were dating, Adaeze spent about three weeks hyping something up like it was going to completely change my life. I knew that if our relationship was going to stand a chance, it was imperative that I take part in this. And what was this huge event?

The release of Beyoncé's *Black Is King* on Disney+.

I had seen the banner advertising it when we pulled up a Marvel movie, but I had no clue what it was about or why it was such a big deal. Adaeze's zeal, however, made it clear that whatever it was, it was important for me to be part of it with her.

That fateful evening, we sat down on the couch, ready for the spectacle to begin. The film opens with Beyoncé walking along a beach in a flowy white dress with some music playing behind her. I quickly realized that this was basically an hour-and-a-half-long music video for the album she had just released. To be honest, I was a little disappointed. I thought it was going to have something to do with *The Lion King*.

A: It did!

C: [Eye roll] Or I thought maybe it would be an exposé on Beyoncé's life behind the scenes while making the album—something like that. No. This was an extended celebration of the art of Beyoncé's music. It had a ton of dancing that seemed strange to me, and some blue dude was sporadically running around, which I never fully understood. I think there was even a baby floating in the clouds at one point—I don't know. I was completely lost, but I knew Adaeze was having the time of her life. So I took it all in.

We had ordered some food to eat during the show. Within fifteen minutes, I was finished, but Adaeze hadn't even touched hers.

A: I had *too* touched my food!

C: Let me tell you something about my wife. She eats in very small bites, and when she's thinking hard about something, she will take one bite about every twenty minutes.

A: So, like I said, I *had* touched my food, thank you very much!

C: So, like *I* said, she still had a whole plate in front of her. The reason I know this is because I leaned back, letting Adaeze's couch swallow me, waiting for her to finish her food and lean back into me as usual. However, she was so locked into what was happening on the screen that she had no idea I had even leaned back. By the time she finally sat back and relaxed, the film had only about ten minutes left.

After it was over, I thought, *Eh, I could take it or leave it.*

But Adaeze refused to even speak until the last credit had rolled and the screen went back to the menu, at which point she turned to me and said emphatically, "That was amazing!"

I thought, *Oh, crap. I'd better change my attitude a little bit.* "Yeah . . . it was really good."

A: I thought it was such a beautiful expression of Black culture—celebrating some of our history, some of where we come from, and specifically Africa, the motherland. I remember having a little twinge in my spirit at the title, *Black Is King,* because I strongly and full-heartedly believe and know that *Jesus* is King . . .

C: Amen!

A: . . . and it felt a little idolatrous for Black culture, or anyone, to say that anyone besides Jesus is king. But I kind of, you know, scooted that aside for the sake of appreciating some art created by a Black woman that was being featured on Disney+. I've never seen a banner that big for something by a Black woman on *any* streaming service, so there were a lot of reasons to feel celebrated. But—peep game—there were some scenes in it that I thought were a little demonic-y.

(Full transparency: I don't listen to Beyoncé anymore for my own personal and spiritual reasons. But at the time, I was full-on both a Beyoncé fan and a fan of this piece of art.)

I was so into it that I don't think I was even aware that Chad wasn't as engaged as I was . . .

C: You had no clue.

A: And I didn't care—I was so enraptured by what we were watching. I loved the freedom being expressed through the people onscreen. Songs like "Brown Skin Girl" celebrated *my* skin in a way I'd never seen on a television screen. Literally every person on the screen was some beautiful shade of brown, from light caramel to almost the deepest black pearl. It was a special thing to behold (even if it was flawed because of certain artistic choices). And it was meaningful to experience it with Chad.

I'll admit, I was today years old when I learned that he had to muster up his excited response! But it also makes me appreciate—even more—the heart of my husband. Once he realizes I'm excited about something, his typical response is "Oh, good to know!" and then he meets me there as best as he can.

That's what it means to celebrate what we don't understand. Chad didn't totally understand the film in the moment or even later, after we had more discussions about why it meant so much to me. But the memory of enjoying that experience with him is forever seared in my mind. It didn't even matter that he wasn't as into it as me. What matters is that he was *there* with me, supporting me, even if it was through silent confusion.

C: That time I got it right. That's not to say I did anything special—I was just sitting there with Adaeze. Interestingly, the memory that sticks out for me is the look on Adaeze's face after we watched it together. It was clear how much it meant that I had watched it with her, despite my lack of understanding of what the movie was all about. The big thing was she didn't feel like I had judged anything or I was downplaying the beauty of what we'd just seen.

A: Or making fun of it.

C: Yeah, I just sat and watched it with her, and she felt celebrated simply because I was present.

THE FLIP SIDE

A: Granted, being physically present with someone isn't always all that's needed for that someone to feel celebrated.

For example, to the utter displeasure of *my* musical taste, Chad loves Dave Matthews Band. He has been to . . . thirty shows?

C: Seventeen . . .

A: I love him anyway.

In 2020, Chad wanted to take me to the Gorge in Washington for back-to-back-to-back shows over all three days of Labor Day weekend. (That's why it's called "Labor Dave" weekend, in case you didn't know—or care.)

I imagine it was the most granola event ever.

C: Oh, it's incredibly crunchy.

A: However, because of COVID-19, it was canceled. So we had to make do with two back-to-back shows the following summer in Colorado.

I was well aware that I would probably be one of the few, if not the *only*, Black person there. I was also aware that my husband had made great memories at these shows over the years with his friends. So I genuinely wanted to go, just to be there for him. However, when Chad played me some of the band's early music, I didn't care for the lead man's singing voice. I thought he sounded like Kermit the Frog. But even though the vocalist in me was unimpressed, the musician in me really appreciated the band and their talent.

C: For the record, I would agree that Dave Matthews is not the best singer of all time, but his band is legitimately incredible.

A: Hear, hear!

C: Also, like a lot of white boys my age, I listened to a lot of Dave Matthews Band in college. So, yes, there's sentimental value there, and I have a long history of listening to their music.

There, I feel fully defended.

A: I agreed to go—and not begrudgingly. I was genuinely down to go with Chad. Never mind that it was on both a Friday *and* Saturday night, and because I was a worship pastor at the time, I had to get up very early for work on Sunday mornings. But a couple from my worship team was there too, and we sat with them both nights, which added an extra level of fun. It didn't hurt that the husband of the couple was in the same shoes as me—not really a fan of Dave but there for his wife, who is as big of a fan as Chad is. It was nice to have some camaraderie in that.

C: I am so proud. You know I made Adaeze into a fan because she called Dave by his first name. Only hard-core Dave fans call Dave *Dave*.

A: Oh, ew.

And also, false. I am no such thing.

Anyway, the first night, as I stood there for hours with my husband, I was having a huge mental war. We were both enjoying the music, but there were some very rude people around us puffing smoke close to our faces. Plus, we were on a hill, and standing on an incline for hours on end got pretty uncomfortable. But my husband wanted to stand the entire evening, so I wanted to stand with him. (Spoiler alert: the second night, I had to sit down, and I fell asleep with my head resting on my knees.)

I felt very alone in that crowd, but I also knew I wasn't there for me. I tried to put on a good face for my husband, but I didn't do the best job of making him feel celebrated that night.

C: I was definitely aware that Adaeze was not loving it *and* that she was a little uncomfortable. I also knew that she was think-ing about having to get up early the next morning. Of course, I really wanted her to have a great time, but the fact that she went with me to both shows meant so much. That was really all I needed.

Will I go to more Dave Matthews Band concerts? Very likely yes.

Will my wife? Very likely no. And I'm okay with that.

I just wanted her to be with me for at least one and give it a try. (Okay, I took her to two back-to-back nights, but that's part of the experience!) Even though she wasn't in perfect spirits about the whole thing, I love that we have that memory.

By the way, if it feels like we're hyper-focusing on times when Adaeze doesn't feel seen or celebrated, the reality is that white people generally *are* seen and celebrated in American culture, and I don't think it's a stretch to say that's true in Western culture in general. So I can feel seen and celebrated at any given moment. However, if Adaeze doesn't feel seen or celebrated when there is a victory in Black culture (like the Beyoncé movie), then I missed an opportunity.

For the record, I took her to another white-boy show that summer, and she rocked her face off for two straight hours.

A: COLONY HOOOOOUSE!!!!!!

C: See? She can get into white-boy music. Dave Matthews just isn't her thing.

C&A: These may seem like silly examples, and admittedly they kind of are, but they show how much it means when you make an effort to celebrate something you may not fully understand—or even like—with a friend of a different race. Sometimes that's what being supportive looks like.

Yes, we're talking about this from a racial reconciliation frame of reference, but really it applies to anyone. You don't have to love the thing as much as the other person does. Simply putting in the effort goes a long way.

Celebrating what someone else loves really has nothing to do with what we personally like. It's about asking ourselves how *we* would want to be celebrated if the situation were flipped. Yes, we might be uncomfortable. However, we might also learn something.

Stepping into interracial relationships of any kind involves going outside what you believe is normal—what revolves around you—and entering someone else's reality.

This is why it's also good to talk about experiences we don't understand (like asking Adaeze what she loved so much about the Beyoncé film or asking Chad about the memories he and his friends had made at other DMB concerts). If you never ask questions or talk about what you don't understand, you'll never learn, the other person won't feel celebrated, and we'll never make any progress.

To quote Dave Matthews, "Don't rob yourself of all that you could be." (We'll just let you guess which one of us thought to include that.)

A lot of times, we stay away from what we don't understand because we're afraid of not doing it right, not understanding it right, or not showing up right—especially when it comes to interracial relationships. However, when we approach what we don't understand with love, we can be humble enough to listen, be corrected, and see the other person for who they are.

The good news is we don't have to be afraid. As 1 John 4:18 says, "There is no fear in love." Love drives away the fear that sometimes debilitates us—the same fear that keeps us from trying. It's not that we'll get it perfect just because we love the other person. We're still going to step in it from time to time. After all, we're human.

But if we're following Jesus' lead, we will learn to love each other and really lean in to see the depths in one another. We will pray for each other and love each other even when someone is not "our own people."

In 1 Peter 3:8, it says, "Be like-minded, be sympathetic, love one another, be compassionate and humble." The easiest way to support somebody we don't fully understand or are nervous about approaching is to follow that verse.

Love one another.

Be sympathetic.

And being like-minded doesn't mean uniformity or agreement about everything but that we try to see things from others' points of view.

If we do those things, we can turn a potentially incendiary conversation on its head.

But if we're failing at making people feel loved, at some point, we gotta start over. How? First, by looking inward and making sure our motives are pure, not selfish. Then, by listening, which includes admitting we don't know everything—nor do we understand everything—and realizing it's okay to learn and grow together.

If we love each other honestly and genuinely, we will naturally exude humility and compassion. Those are disarming traits to have—especially when someone's blowing smoke in your face at a Dave Mathews Band concert.

CHAPTER 11

DOWN THE RABBIT HOLE

C: When it comes to entering into each other's mud, there are three things we consider to be keys to success. I wouldn't go so far as to say they are silver bullets—nothing is truly a silver bullet.

Except in vampire stories.

There are silver bullets in those.

A: [Shakes head, drops head to hands, holding back laughter.]

C: First—and we've learned this the hard way—in order to develop genuine interracial relationships, you have to earn each other's trust. Actually, I should have just said, "We've learned," because there really is no easy way to earn someone's trust—at least not fully or to the depth needed to sit with each other in the mess.

A: Trust isn't something that happens overnight. It takes time—quality time, intentional time. When we want someone to trust us, it seems like it should just be given. We know our intentions. We know what's behind our words and actions. And because those intentions are obvious to us, we assume others should automatically give us the benefit of the doubt. But to the one expected to *give* trust, the feeling is more like, "Prove to me that you are worthy of my trust," especially if that person has been hurt before. And especially if that hurt has come from someone who has the same skin tone as the one who is now expecting trust.

One of the ways Chad earned my trust was by standing up for our relationship. Right from the beginning, he didn't shy away from having tough conversations with his family when needed. And when things got tough because of the judgment and opinions coming at us from the outside, he didn't run away. He pressed in and was man enough to sit with me through it all.

My trust wasn't always the easiest thing for him to earn either. My trust had been taken advantage of and tossed to the side like a used napkin in previous interracial relationships, and I've had friends give up on our friendship after a misunderstanding lasted a little too long for their liking. The fact that Chad hung in there with me and was willing to work through our misunderstandings was meaningful proof that he was a man of his word.

C: One of the ways Adaeze earned my trust was by letting me fail. I never felt judged by her when I didn't get things right. Instead, she was patient with me and let me grow without the expectation of being perfect. She showed patience when I was oblivious during interactions with cashiers who completely ignored her presence when we checked out. She was patient with me as I grew more aware of the stares around us, and she gave me grace for the times I missed them. She was also patient as I learned how to direct attention away from myself so she could be treated as my equal and as the beautiful human she is. And she commended me for trying even when I didn't do it perfectly.

I HEAR YOU ...

A: The second key is listening. We will never truly understand one another if we don't listen. Listening with an open heart always leads to a deeper understanding of the other person—and ourselves.

C: When we first started dating, our trust was fragile, which is why Adaeze would sometimes shut down, and I would feel like I had to walk on eggshells. Initially I was more worried about getting my point across and being heard than listening to Adaeze. Now I am better at listening first and then responding. Our trust has grown to the point that, when we miss each other, we know we can revisit the topic and get back on the same page.

When we talk about listening, we don't just mean hearing the words people say to you. Sometimes listening means paying attention to the things that are not actually spoken, like when Adaeze rolls her eyes at me, physically turns away from me, or shuts down and goes off by herself. I could take that personally, or I could listen to what Adaeze's response is telling me about how safe—or unsafe—I am making her feel. Kind of like the headwrap incident. Adaeze might not have verbalized her frustration with me, but her silence and body language spoke volumes. Really knowing someone means taking the time to learn their nonverbal clues so you can keep the lines of communication open, even when emotions are running too hot to be put into words.

A: I've learned that one of Chad's nonverbal cues is shutting down, both physically and verbally. He has a history of being treated as though his opinions and feelings don't matter or aren't wanted, so he can feel like that's what I'm doing if I'm not listening to him well. So when Chad's "Okay" is short and followed by silence or when he physically distances himself from me or when he makes himself physically smaller by folding his hands and sitting deeper into his seat, I know I've missed him somewhere. And when Chad is frustrated, usually because I've given him reason to believe he's on his own to crack the case on whatever "misunderstandment" (as I call them) we're having, he'll pick at his manly eyebrows in a disgruntled manner or run his hands through his hair. That's my cue to slow down, reassure him that we're in this together, gently offer our shared love language of physical touch, and try to come at the problem from a different angle.

I FEEL YOU...

C: The third key is empathy. When I was in physical therapy school, we talked a lot about empathy. The metaphor we worked from was that having empathy is similar to climbing into a rabbit hole with the person and, to the best of our ability, attempting to feel right alongside them. This is different from sympathy, which looks more like shouting condolences down from the outside.

Doing life with Adaeze has given me a new understanding of the implications of the rabbit hole. For Adaeze, and for any person of color, her life will be spent in this rabbit hole. Unless society changes and racism and oppression are rendered obsolete, the Black community will remain trapped in this hole.

As a white man, I can empathize all I want, but no matter how deep I go into this rabbit hole, I will never fully understand her experience. And as much as it pains me to admit it, at the end of the day, I am part of the system that dug the hole in the first place.

During the summer of 2020, when social unrest was at its peak, Adaeze was really struggling. I kind of understood, but I didn't really get it. Not the way she did. I could hear about a Black man I didn't know being shot and get over it with a, "That's so sad," because it was not my reality. For Adaeze, however, it was a stifling reminder of the way the world is constantly slanted against her.

A: That summer was one of the darkest seasons of my life. Not just because of the unexpected intensity of the racial unrest but also because of the tension from Chad's family and the ongoing issues at work. All the injustice, all the innocent Black people dying, pushed me to the edge. I began to think, *I don't wanna live in a world where this is my reality.*

I felt like the Israelites wandering in the wilderness for forty years—only this felt like a never-ending wilderness of racism that had been here long before me and seemed like it would be here long after me. It was as if every time I found some light, another engulfing wave of darkness would hit via another shooting or hashtag. On top of that, I was surrounded by white people at work who either were acting like it wasn't a big deal or were only then, after six years, inviting me into their homes to "check on me." Being suddenly invited into the home of someone who had never pursued relational depth with me before felt ingenuine, even if it was genuine. It seemed performative or like an overextension. I appreciated the sentiment, but it just drove home the reality I was facing.

I would think, *What's the point of fighting racism if it will never end? If even the people I thought were my friends still say and laugh at the N-word?*

One day I posted a picture of myself on social media wearing a sweatshirt that had "BLACK POWER" written across it in bright, colorful letters, with a caption about Black lives mattering being the minimum. Soon after, Chad told me about someone in his family having an issue with my post. Since when does stating that my Black life matters, especially in a world where I've been made to feel otherwise, mean that no one else's life matters? Just because I celebrate being Black and attempt to reclaim some of the identity and autonomy that were stripped from Black people doesn't mean I hate those who are white. It is, literally and figuratively, not that black and white.

It seemed like nothing I was doing was making a difference—in my workplace, in my neighborhood, or with my future family-in-law.

Racial tension was coming at me from every angle, and no one seemed to understand. It felt like nobody around me was seeing things from my point of view. People just kept telling me, "You are so strong. Just keep going," and I didn't feel like I could talk to anyone about it except my Black friends. But since they were all going through the same kind of stuff, I didn't want to add to their load by sharing mine.

I felt so helpless. I just wanted to be done with the fight and be in heaven with Jesus and my daddy. Initially, I didn't explain all this to Chad, which was a mistake.

One night we were sitting on his couch, and I suddenly reached over and hugged him. Holding him tight, I said, "I love you."

C: I knew what that "I love you" meant. We had been in a relationship long enough that I recognized Adaeze's tone. The way she hugged me this time felt different. I boldly asked, "Did you just say goodbye to me?"

There was no dialogue for a while. Adaeze just sobbed in my arms, validating my question.

We sat there for at least ten minutes. Finally, Adaeze broke the silence. She started telling me some of what she'd been feeling, all of which underscored that this was not just "a passing moment" for people of color. The rabbit hole is deep, and there doesn't seem to be any way out.

As our relationship progressed, I realized that in order for me to fully empathize with Adaeze, I needed to come to grips with the fact that I would never fully understand her reality because it is not my reality. We've all been there when a person says, "I understand," in response to whatever we're going through, when in reality they have no idea. Inevitably, we just want to slap the person for saying they get it when we both know they don't.

In these moments, our best course of action is to lean into Paul's advice. In Romans 12:15, he writes, "Rejoice with those who rejoice, weep with those who weep. Live in harmony with one another" (ESV). Even though I may not be able to fully understand what Adaeze is feeling or experiencing, I can still rejoice with her when good things—like the Beyoncé documentary—happen, and I can still sit in that rabbit hole with her, listen to her, and hold her while she cries it out so she doesn't feel like she's going through it alone.

A: Being with someone like Chad, who isn't trying to escape or avoid my rabbit-hole experience, makes all the difference in our relationship. I'm able to share my feelings and experiences even if he won't ever feel or experience them in my shoes. It would be much too easy to retreat into myself and lock Chad out, but I can't expect him to understand how I'm feeling if I'm not willing to get real with him about it.

C & A: If we open up to each other about whatever rabbit holes we find ourselves in and listen with the intent of understanding instead of just responding, the differences that people outside the relationship see as "problems" will only make us stronger. This is why it's even more important for us to be open and real with each other about how we feel.

A: For example, I will never forget what Chad told me in the car on the way to the grocery store. We were talking about something that had to do with a couple of our friends, a white male and a Black female.

After we'd disagreed for a bit, Chad told me, "I don't feel like I can voice my opinion in defense of him, for fear that it will come across like I'm only defending him because *I'm* a white male."

He also confessed to me that sometimes he doesn't feel like he can speak into race issues with me because he doesn't want to come across like the privileged white male who, of course, will side with the white person in question.

That got to me. That definitely isn't the way I want him to feel when it comes to talking about race issues with me—ever. Whether I had given him that impression or not, I was happy he told me about it so I could speak truth from my perspective:

his voice and opinion *always* matter to me, and he's not just my *white* husband. He's my husband—PERIODT, with a *t*!

To me, that means his word always counts, even if we disagree about the matter at hand.

Chad and I have learned and relearned that we don't have to agree on every single thing, even when it comes to race. As Robert Jones Jr. has been quoted as saying, "We can disagree and still love each other, unless your disagreement is rooted in my oppression and denial of my humanity and right to exist." This is not an excuse for cancel culture, and just because it was said by a Black man doesn't mean it's exclusive to Black people. I need to give Chad the same respect, love, and empathy I need from him.

In that sense, the rabbit-hole analogy can go both ways, in that I cannot for a moment think that *my* rabbit hole or *my* experience is more important than Chad's just because of the histories of our different races. Sure, people usually talk about the rabbit hole in relation to things that are painful, and in that sense, the Black experience seems like the more natural fit. At the same time, I imagine it can feel kind of like a game of The Floor is Lava for a white person to try to understand my Black experience. They're trying to figure out where it's safe to step and where it's not and what's okay to say or ask while avoiding land mines. This doesn't negate my feelings, but it's important for me to be aware of the other person's perspective.

C: God gave me a wife who is one of the most graceful and humble women I have ever met. It means so much to me that, in racial conversations, she wants to hear what I'm thinking and feeling, even when she's the one hurting. Like a lot of white people, I sometimes feel totally inadequate talking about race, especially when that conversation involves a person of color. I don't want to abuse the grace she extends to me. It's my job to realize where the lava is, and once I've found it, to not continue to step in it. This is why we need to get comfortable in the rabbit hole and learn as much as we can about said lava.

A: By the way, it's zero fun feeling like people think I'm making Chad stay in the rabbit hole with me. This has been a rebuttal we've faced when Chad has stood up for me.

For one thing, I'm not.

For another, that assumption dishonors the beauty of our relationship and Chad's strength to take up the torch on my behalf.

C: Likewise, I hate that Adaeze sometimes feels like she's a burden or that she's somehow making me join her in her rabbit hole against my will. Just for total clarity: she is not.

Also, I hope this is obvious, but white people need to carry this same grace into conversations about race. It is a lot easier to give a person the benefit of the doubt when mistakes are made by someone who has shown you dignity and respect.

Any given conversation about race can be triggering to a person of color—for a multitude of reasons. That's why we need to remember that we don't know what the person we're talking to has been through. Any response toward us that's less than ideal is likely representative of a recurring trigger for that person.

For example, one morning we needed to get up for church, but my alarm didn't go off. Adaeze knew that I needed to wake up, so she turned on the bedroom lights. All of a sudden, the back of my eyelids changed from black to a bright red-orange.

I was shook.

I jolted awake, and—embarrassingly—the first emotion I felt was anger. I didn't snap at Adaeze, but I was not the most pleasant person in the world either. What Adaeze didn't know was that, when I was growing up, my mom used to do the exact same thing when she needed to get me out of bed quickly—and I hated it.

So my frustration had less to do with Adaeze and more to do with my conditioning to hastily hop into fresh underwear and get going after being jarred awake by lights first thing in the morning. Granted, this example is very much apples to oranges in light of the injustices Adaeze has had to deal with, but it does show how seemingly benign comments or questions can result in explosive reactions.

A more pointed example is the panic attack Adaeze suffered at the idea of going to see my grandparents in Virginia. I was neglecting the fact that, for Adaeze, the trip represented so much more than just meeting my grandparents. So when I said, "Well, we just need to go," she felt completely abandoned. My lack of understanding made the darkness of her rabbit hole feel even more suffocating—hence the panic attack. That's not to say that if I'd been more empathetic the whole episode could have been avoided, but it would have at least helped her feel less alone.

C & A: Speaking of empathy . . . know what the shortest verse in the Bible is?

"Jesus wept" (John 11:35).

It's such a simple sentence, yet it carries massive weight. Jesus was fully human and fully God, and He felt every bit of the pain and emotion we feel. Jesus had just lost one of His closest friends. The image of Jesus sitting with us in our struggles is the ultimate example of the way we're supposed to live. Jesus fully embodied the kind of empathy and compassion we're called to have.

Jesus' followers did the same. Throughout Paul's letters, he teaches about empathy. A classic example is in Romans 12:10: "Love one another with brotherly affection" (ESV). In other words, we serve the Lord by outdoing each other in love.

Likewise, we're challenged in 1 Peter 4:8-9 to "keep loving one another earnestly, since love covers a multitude of sins" and to "show hospitality to one another without grumbling" (ESV).

Simply put, our job as followers of Christ is to welcome all people without judgment and to put the love of God on full display in every interaction. We're called to a higher level of unity, which is achieved by showing abundant love.

Before He was betrayed, Jesus prayed for His followers, "[May they] all be one, just as You, Father, are in Me, and I in You, that they also may be in Us, so that the world may believe that You have sent Me. The glory that You have given Me I have given to them, that they may be one even as We are one" (John 17:21-22, ESV). Jesus wants us to all be unified in our devotion to God the Father and to our brothers and sisters in Christ. We are first His, and we identify as His *together*.

Paul reiterates this idea in Galatians 3:28: "There is neither slave nor free, there is no male and female, for you are all one in Christ Jesus" (ESV). One of the most revealing passages on the topic of unity is 1 Corinthians 12, where Paul describes the body of Christ. We'll keep this short because you really should go read it for yourself. The gist is that each part of the body of Christ (male, female, Black, white, Brown, rich, poor, Seahawks fans, or 49ers fans) has a part to play in God's sovereign plan, and the body works best when all parts are functioning together.

In other words, we all need each other. That's why we need to take the time to listen, learn from each other, and consider a perspective that is different from our own—and every bit as valuable.

Getting involved in interracial relationships won't necessarily end racism. But when both parties know who they are individually and understand the implications of the relationship they're stepping into, these relationships can be a force to be reckoned with.

Ultimately, this is a journey. We all need to be ready to take the slow, narrow path toward healing. The best way to start is to follow the example laid out by Jesus: loving the Lord with all our heart, mind, and strength, and loving our neighbor as ourselves (Mark 12:30-31). When this is our foundation, we can begin the work of being truly unified under Christ.

That's the only way the walls that currently divide us will come down. Then and only then will we be a strong community of diverse followers of Christ with different strengths and weaknesses, complementing one another in a way that only the Lord could piece together.

Thanks for rocking with us throughout this journey.

Now, without further ado, we'd like to share the rest of that headwrap story with you.

THE OTHER FIVE WORDS THAT CHANGED EVERYTHING

✦ ✦ ✦ ✦ ✦ ✦ ✦ ✦ ✦ ✦ ✦ ✦ ✦ ✦ ✦ ✦

C: The fact that my comment about Adaeze's headwrap had her questioning our entire relationship made me realize that as close as I *thought* we were, I really had no idea what she was thinking or where she was coming from.

All I knew for sure was that I didn't want to lose her—especially over a comment that I thought showed her how much I cared about her.

Completely lost, I finally said, "Okay, babe, can you please help me understand what those looks in the brewery meant to you?

A: *Finally, he's asking to understand my reality and not just trying to get me to exist in his.*

"Thank you for asking that. The thing is—I don't know for

sure what all those looks meant. Is it because I'm Black? Is it because they see me as less than? Those looks could have meant a lot of different things. But any way you look at it, they were coming at me because, in a room like that, I am seen as different.

"So when you said, 'It's just people looking,' it felt like you were downplaying my feelings because those looks don't hit you the same way they hit me. In those situations, it would help me feel less alone if, instead of defending or explaining away why people are looking at us, you're more aware of the position those looks put me in, and you give me the space to feel differently about it than you do. That's why I was asking whether you're aware of my reality as a Black woman."

C: "That's fair. And you're right. I hadn't considered how a situation like that would make you feel."

For the record, the point I had been trying to make with my headwrap comment—and still stand by—was that I was ready for whatever was to come. I was proud to be with Adaeze for *all* of her. Her headwrap was a physical display of her culture. I was attempting to let her know that I understood our worlds were different and that being in a relationship with her meant my world would be different. I was trying to tell her that I wanted to step into her world with her.

A: A whole new wooooorld . . . ! (You're welcome, *Aladdin* fans.)

C: [Laughs and shakes head.] But when I pointed at her headwrap and uttered those fateful five words, "Even when you're wearing that," what she essentially heard was, "I know you're different, but I don't care."

The only thing that might have been worse is if I had said

something totally cliché, like "All the things that make you different make you beautiful."

A: Gross.

C: Either way, all she was hearing was, "You're different." And historically, for Adaeze, that meant "less than."

A: I *thought* I understood what he meant by the headwrap comment, but clearly I didn't, so we both missed each other a little there.

"I want us to be on the same page, though. I don't want our different experiences to come between us."

C: "I agree. I'm sorry I wasn't more aware of what was going on. I really do want to be more aware of how you're feeling in those situations so you don't feel isolated."

A: "I really appreciate that. And your willingness to try really does mean a lot."

C: We walked around and continued to talk for almost two hours, and then we found a bench under a tree so we could sit down and rest our legs. It was a beautiful evening. The night sky was perfectly clear. We could even see some stars poking through the metro Denver area haze.

A: I leaned back on the bench, Chad put his arm around my shoulders, and we stared up at the stars, relaxing in the knowledge that we now had a much better understanding between us. I felt heard, and I felt like I was able to hear Chad better too.

Overall, I was in a much different headspace than I had been two hours earlier, in part because Chad had listened to me and validated how I felt. I had half-expected him to say, "You're right. This *is* too much." Instead, not only was he still there, but he was no longer trying to defend his position. He was genuinely invested in understanding mine and in learning what he could do differently. He was even affirming me, and that was hugely disarming.

I didn't say much on that bench. I just stared at the stars, listened as Chad said some very sweet things, and took it all in. Then he said . . .

C: "You know, there is a reason we can have conversations like this and I *still* want to hang out with you under the stars. There's a reason you make me laugh more than anyone else I've been around. There's a reason I get so excited every time I see you. There's a reason I want to make sure you don't run away when we miss each other in tough conversations. There's a reason I want to have difficult conversations with my family about our relationship. There's a reason I want to share you with the world but also hold you tight and not share you with anyone . . ."

A: I could hardly believe it. All I could think was, *He's still sitting here with me. He isn't running away. He doesn't want to leave. He didn't say he's done for the night. Is this really happening? Is he really saying all this after we just talked about all that difficult stuff? What is happening?*

C: "There's a reason I will walk with you for two hours to have a conversation we need to have. There's a reason I will sit shivering in the cold night air on a bench with you under the stars. There's a reason I want to sit with you for hours on an unsanded bench that's giving me splinters in awkward places."

A: We cracked up at those last two. I mean, the man says he's not much of a romantic, but sitting there under the stars and listening to him say all those incredibly sweet things was very, very romantic. Eventually my erratic thoughts stilled, and I relaxed into the unforced genuineness of Chad vulnerably sharing how he felt about me.

C: "Are you still staring at the stars?"

A: "Yes!" I replied, smiling but not breaking my upward gaze.

I *had* been pretty lost in the stars. All I could think was, *This is perfect. Don't look at him or scare him off. Let him talk. Just be here in the moment.* Ironic, huh? I was trying to be in the moment with Chad so much that I barely even looked at him.

Then Chad raised his hand to my chin and gently turned my face toward him. Our eyes met for the first time since we'd sat down. He paused for a second, gazed into my eyes, then borderline yelled, "I freaking love you, Adaeze!"

He brought my face to his and kissed me.

It was perfect.

C: I had been trying to find a time to tell Adaeze that I loved her that whole week, but the perfect moment never came. I was starting to think it wouldn't happen, so . . . I just let 'er rip.

Ironically, or perhaps perfectly, it came at a time when vulnerability was at its peak between us. I had proven to be totally unprepared for what we were stepping into, but I was still crazy about Adaeze. I still wanted more.

A: Let me tell you, "I love you" is one thing. "I *freaking* love you" just hits different. The desperation, rawness, and almost recklessness the word *freaking* injects into what's being expressed seems braver and wilder than a simple "I love you." The stakes seem higher—as does the possible fall from the risk of rejection. With everything we'd been through in our relationship, "freaking" was like an act of defiance. In the face of the racism we'd dealt with, one could wonder *how* Chad found himself loving me. "Freaking" answered that. There he was, bold enough not only to embrace his feelings for me but to loudly declare them into the night sky.

The audacity.

Since Chad kissed me before I could respond, after our kiss, I reciprocated. "Freaking" and all.

In the course of one evening, we had gone from arguing over headwraps to professing our love for each other. Looking back, I realize I was so fixated on the stars because I was still insecure from being told so often that I was "too much" because of the way I talked about racial stuff. This insecurity made me unsure where this conversation would end up. Truth be told, it was mind-boggling to me that after everything I'd said, he was still there next to me. I wasn't used to that.

Having Chad tell me he loved me hushed all the fears that he didn't get it and that we were too different. When he borderline shouted those five beautiful words at me, I realized this was a man who, as much as he could at this point in our relationship, saw me for everything I was.

I'd just spent two hours being real with him about who

I was and how I saw things, and he was *still* crazy about me. The way he fought for me that night caught me completely by surprise—yet somehow didn't surprise me at all.

C: It's wild to think that I'd almost ended things with Adaeze that day with five poorly chosen words, but a few hours later, five more carefully chosen words gave us a whole new beginning.

A: That was one way Chad led me into pretty unchartered territory. As if telling me, "I freaking love you!" wasn't enough, he followed it by holding my face in his hands and telling me, "I'm not going anywhere. It doesn't matter how many walks we need, we will fight for each other, and I will always be here."

I believed him.

And I still do.

C & A: The whole headwrap incident, as painful as it was, taught us both a valuable lesson. Both sides carry a certain amount of responsibility in a relationship. One side needs to ask, listen, and learn, and the other needs to be willing to give the benefit of the doubt, extend grace, and try to understand when mistakes are made.

On both of our parts, there were plenty of mistakes, uncomfortable silences, and tears. But there were also smiles and laughs, and through all of it, there was love.

That conversation was just the beginning of us getting on the same page with each other. We still had a long way to go and a lot of long, hard conversations in our future. But this one proved to us that we would be able to get on the same page because now we knew we were wearing the same jerseys. We were willing to fight for each other. We could get in the dirt together, have the hard conversations, and come out better and closer in the end.

That's what it's all about—deciding that you care enough about each other to get down in the dirt and wrestle your way through the missteps and misunderstandings, flybys and false assumptions, slipups and stereotypes, and well-intentioned yet wounding comments *together*. The more you show a genuine willingness to listen, learn, and grow in understanding, the more trust will grow.

It doesn't matter what kind of relationship you're in—romantic, platonic, friends, coworkers, in-laws, neighbors—love and respect are love and respect. When Jesus told us to love our neighbor as ourselves, He said the central issue isn't about who our neighbor is—it's being a good neighbor to everyone (Mark 12:31). Our neighbor is whoever God is calling us to love. And God calls us to love everyone, no matter how different they may be from us.

A: If you've been labeled "different," remember that you were created in God's image, and you are His masterpiece. That means you have all the permission you need to celebrate everything that makes you *you*. So it's not just *okay* to love yourself. Jesus literally expects you to—as much as you love others! So go on witcha bad self! Be your biggest fan. And spread that self-love on to others.

Having tough conversations about race, acknowledging our own blind spots, and having enough humility, patience, compassion, and understanding to foster stronger, healthier interracial relationships isn't always easy—or pretty. But we can promise you this: it's totally freaking worth it.

ENCOURAGEMENT FOR THOSE DEALING WITH CHURCH TRAUMA

A: In chapter 6, I shared a very painful part of my story in hopes that it will not only help me continue to heal but help others with the painful parts of their own stories. I've been told too many similar stories by Black people to think that I am alone in this.

When I decided to leave that church, I had no idea how long it'd take me to be completely free from the pain of that experience. It's kind of ridiculous how many times I've attempted to talk about what I went through without actually talking about it. Church trauma can be so difficult to discuss, especially when you've been told by the inflictors of your trauma that what you went through doesn't warrant that label.

Church trauma is not something "church people" like to talk about. It's easier to just sweep it under the rug for fear that it will make the church or those involved look bad. But I've learned there's so much healing and restoration that can be experienced in simply saying what happened.

I don't wanna be guilty of not talking about church trauma or racial trauma—or of not making space for others to do the same. Since nobody I know of is preaching about it . . . here are five things I've learned about trauma:

1. Not talking about it isn't healthy! There's no growth in pretending everything is fine when it's not.

2. Everyone will have an opinion on who you should and shouldn't talk to about it. This is where you get to practice discernment and ask for the Holy Spirit's guidance for when to speak up and when to "just won't."

3. The church is wildly imperfect (myself included), but it's not hopeless.

4. God's grace is boundless, all the time—both for us when we're hurt in our trauma and forget to show grace, and for those who we expect grace from but don't show it.

5. There's an art to peeling the masking tape of tidy "churchiness" from your mouth. As a friend once told me, "Everything said should be true, but not everything true needs to be said."

Whatever your trauma, I hope you let the Lord be your path to healing. It's not an easy road, and I wouldn't be standing today without people in my life who are both objective and safe.

So here's one "church" person choosing to talk about it in an attempt to empower you. Don't let your trauma isolate you!

DISCUSSION QUESTIONS

C & A: These reflective prompts and conversation starters are intended to help you dig deeper into the ideas presented in this book and apply them to your own life and relationships. Feel free to use these questions individually or with a group.

PROLOGUE: THE FIVE WORDS THAT CHANGED EVERYTHING

Adaeze and Chad talk about "the five words that changed everything" in their relationship.

1. As you think about relationships in your life with people who are different from you, what conversations or experiences stand out as defining moments?

2. What made those specific conversations or experiences so significant?

3. What comments or events set your relationship on a different course, and why did they have that effect?

CHAPTER 1: AS DIFFERENT AS BLACK AND WHITE

In this chapter, Adaeze and Chad talk about their upbringing, their families of origin, the communities they grew up in, and how those factors influenced their understanding of race.

1. What were some of the influences that informed your view of race and what was "normal"?

2. How have those influences affected the way you see those around you? Which of those influences are worth challenging or unlearning?

3. In what ways might you be privileged, and how does that influence the way you interact with those around you?

4. Think back to situations where you felt uncomfortable about someone's ignorant comment or question. How would you react differently than you did then?

CHAPTER 2: LET THE AWKWARD CONVERSATIONS BEGIN!

At the end of the chapter, the authors say, "Overcoming past hurts and prejudices takes time. It takes patience. It takes understanding. And it takes a willingness to stay in the fight even if you get a little bruised and bloodied in the process."

1. How have you found this to be true in your life?

2. How willing are you to enter into awkward conversations?

3. What holds you back from engaging, and what are the rewards of doing so?

4. Think back to times when you entered into conflict with another person. What is an example of a conflict that ended in unity? What is an example of a conflict that ended in division?

5. What was the difference between these two conflicts?

CHAPTER 3: DOES EVERYTHING HAVE TO BE ABOUT RACE?

In this chapter, Chad and Adaeze give some examples of the ways they experience situations in different ways and how the world around them reacts to them differently as an interracial couple.

1. As you walk through your daily routines and interact with others, how aware are you of the role race plays?

2. How do you think that level of awareness might differ for someone of another race?

3. What are some interactions you've had in the past that you wish you could change after reading the stories in this chapter?

4. How would you change them?

CHAPTER 4: UNDER THE INFLUENCE

In this chapter, Chad gives us a peek into his own ignorance about how surrounded he was by whiteness, and Adaeze shows how she struggled with the weight of being the only representative of Blackness in Chad's life. These stories end in a call to diversify influences in your life, both socially and through the media we consume.

1. As you evaluate your entertainment sources, what trends do you notice?

2. How might you be intentional about diversifying your music, shows, and social media?

3. Who in your life could you get to know more but haven't yet?

4. Could the reason you haven't taken that leap be because of their differences?

5. How would you approach diversifying your spheres of influence?

CHAPTER 5: EXCUSE ME, BUT I THINK YOU JUST STEPPED IN SOMETHING

In this chapter, Chad and Adaeze talk about blind spots—hurtful things we think, say, and do out of ignorance. At the end of the chapter, they talk about how it's not the worst thing in the world to be ignorant, but it's what we do out of our ignorance that can be positive or negative.

1. Think about the times when your ignorance has been pointed out or revealed to you. Did you respond poorly, with your walls immediately rising, or were you open to learning and growth? Why was that?

2. Describe a time you "stepped in it" and said something that was inadvertently offensive or insulting to a person of another race.

3. Reflect on a time someone said something offensive to you.

4. How did the scenario play out?

5. How did you feel afterward?

CHAPTER 6: TRYING TO BE THE PERFECT BLACK PERSON

In this chapter, Adaeze "goes there" in sharing how she navigated a painful exit from her church. She discusses living with the constant "perfect Black person" expectation and comes to the understanding that she gets to choose when she will or will not engage in tough racial conversations.

1. In your experience, how has the Church handled racial differences?

2. Why do you think so many churches struggle in this area?

3. What's one thing you can do to help make your church a place that better reflects the beauty and diversity of God's Kingdom?

4. Where might you need to reassess your boundaries and release yourself from the expectation to always be teaching, explaining, and correcting when it comes to racial conversations and find your "I just won't"?

5. How do you think society would define the "perfect Black person"?

CHAPTER 7: TRYING TO BE THE PERFECT WHITE PERSON

In this chapter, Chad shares the pressure he feels to be a perfect white person. This pressure threatens to divide him and Adaeze, and they discuss how they learned to move past it together.

1. How would society define the "perfect white person"?

2. In what ways have you experienced or watched someone else experience the pressure of those expectations?

3. How have you dealt with that pressure, both positively and negatively?

4. In what situations can you show more grace for people around you?

CHAPTER 8: GETTING ON THE SAME TEAM

In this chapter, Chad and Adaeze lay out the process of learning how to become a family despite difficult beginnings. Sometimes time heals all wounds, but sometimes it takes time *and* showing up.

1. In what ways does your origin story affect you today?

2. What beliefs and postures have influenced your assumptions?

3. Have you ever confronted a family member about a racially-charged topic? If so, what happened? If not, why not?

4. Are there any relationships you have given up on because they got tiring? Do you think it's possible you gave up prematurely?

CHAPTER 9: PLEASE STOP SAYING, "I DON'T SEE COLOR"

In this chapter, the authors say, "Being 'colorblind' and ignoring our differences rather than celebrating them isn't the answer. The answer is treating people who look different from you with respect."

1. Why do you think people say they don't see color?

2. What is the problem with that sentiment?

3. In what ways does your "family filter" affect the way you see the world around you?

4. How have you not acknowledged someone else's family filter? How might that affect your interactions with that person?

CHAPTER 10: CELEBRATING WHAT WE DON'T UNDERSTAND

In this chapter, Adaeze and Chad share about their *Black Is King* and Dave Matthews Band experiences.

1. When was a time you went outside your preferences or tastes to celebrate what you didn't understand?

2. When was a time someone did this for you? How did it make you feel?

3. When was a time you failed to do this for someone else? How did it make you feel?

4. When was a time someone failed to do this for you? How did it make you feel?

CHAPTER 11: DOWN THE RABBIT HOLE

In this chapter, Chad and Adaeze talk about three keys to cultivate interracial relationships: building trust, listening, and showing empathy.

1. Which one of these comes most naturally to you? Which one is the most challenging?

2. When was a time one of these factors helped build a bridge in a relationship? When was a time the lack of one of these factors burned a bridge?

EPILOGUE: THE OTHER FIVE WORDS THAT CHANGED EVERYTHING

Interracial relationships come with challenges, but they are, as the Brinkmans say, "totally freaking worth it."

1. What are the benefits of entering these difficult conversations and being in relationship with people who are different from us?

2. What are some takeaways you've gleaned from this book?

3. What's one thing that will change in the way you relate to people of different races after reading this book?

SOME OF OUR FAVORITE VERSES

These are some of the verses we've found most helpful and convicting when it comes to interracial relationships—and relationships in general. As you think about what God may be calling you to do in your relationships with coworkers, friends, or family, let these verses wash over you and fill you.

Feel free to snap a photo of these verses to keep on your phone to revisit when you need to be reminded of them. Or you could copy some of them onto index cards to place around your home, in your car, or at your desk. This is a simple way to let the Word of God be alive and active in your life. We pray that the Holy Spirit speaks through them in the way only He can.

- Proverbs 15:1: A gentle answer turns away wrath, but a harsh word stirs up anger.
- Proverbs 12:16: Fools show their annoyance at once, but the prudent overlook an insult.
- Proverbs 11:11: Through the blessing of the upright a city is exalted, but by the mouth of the wicked it is destroyed.
- Proverbs 11:2: When pride comes, then comes disgrace, but with humility comes wisdom.

- Proverbs 16:24: Gracious words are a honeycomb, sweet to the soul and healing to the bones.
- Proverbs 16:32: Better a patient person than a warrior, one with self-control than one who takes a city.
- Proverbs 17:17: A friend loves at all times, and a brother is born for a time of adversity.
- Proverbs 18:13: To answer before listening—that is folly and shame.
- Proverbs 18:21: The tongue has the power of life and death, and those who love it will eat its fruit.
- Proverbs 20:12: Ears that hear and eyes that see—the LORD has made them both.
- Proverbs 21:21: Whoever pursues righteousness and love finds life, prosperity and honor.
- Proverbs 21:23: Those who guard their mouths and their tongues keep themselves from calamity.
- Proverbs 22:11: One who loves a pure heart and who speaks with grace will have the king for a friend.
- Proverbs 24:3-4: By wisdom a house is built, and through understanding it is established; through knowledge its rooms are filled with rare and beautiful treasures.
- Proverbs 27:17: As iron sharpens iron, so one person sharpens another.
- Proverbs 28:1: The wicked flee though no one pursues, but the righteous are as bold as a lion.
- Proverbs 29:20: Do you see someone who speaks in haste? There is more hope for a fool than for them.
- James 1:19-20, ESV: Know this, my beloved brothers: let every person be quick to hear, slow to speak, slow to anger; for the anger of man does not produce the righteousness of God.

ACKNOWLEDGMENTS

A book like this doesn't happen in isolation, and we wanna give credit where credit is due, with immense gratitude.

First off, we need to thank our families for sticking with us through this process.

To the Azubuike side of the family, thank you for being a safe space for us to be our true selves. You are a beautiful example of bringing a bit of heaven to earth in the way you celebrate differences and allow those differences to be an opportunity for learning how to love those around us better. We love that we can go from goofy running-with-jokes together to theological conversations to talking things out, all within a matter of minutes, and still all like each other in the end. You all are truly a blessing to us.

To the Brinkman side of the family, thank you all for engaging with us in the way you have. Some people would have walked away when the conversations began to get tough, but you all have done the opposite and leaned in. Through it all, we are family, and that will always be true. Thank you for being constant and wanting the best for us. Your trust through this process as we talked about difficulties from the past allowed us to speak honestly and help others along a journey to unity and healing. We are honored to call you family and have you behind us.

To our friends who sat with us, whether in monthly hangs at local spots or in our home, you helped fill us and our home with love, laughter, and truth. You were some of the first eyes on our book cover, some of the first ears to the stories that fill its pages, and some of the first prayer warriors as we began this journey years ago. Thank you for being in our corner.

To everyone who has invited us to their podcasts, to their conferences, and to their events leading up to this book, thank you for sowing into this book without even knowing it.

To anyone who has engaged with the things we post on social media, especially those who have encouraged us to continue using our voices, thank you for letting the Lord use ya!

We were blessed to work with the best team God could have picked out specially for us. Tyndale, *thank you* seems small for how grateful we are that you took a chance on a couple of newbie writers answering the call to write their first book together. We know there are many people behind the Tyndale scenes who we may not have met yet and still championed our book. We appreciate the Tyndale Momentum team!

Special thanks to Kara Leonino, the baddest Senior Acquisitions Editor to roam the earth. Thank you for following the prompting of the Holy Spirit to reach out to us in November 2020 during such a wild and painful time in our lives. Your attention to detail and your tenacity to ask strangers brave questions like, "Does writing a book even interest you?" are some of the many things that make you not only great at what you do for a living but also an absolute gem of a human. You win all informative voice messages battles. Ramen and speakeasies in Denver look good on you, and we're thankful that you're now stuck with us as friends for life. Not sorry.

Carol Traver, Madam Senior Development Editor, who would

probably roll her eyes at our use of *Madam* but also effortlessly deserves it, thank you for putting up with every moment of ridiculousness from us while being such a blast to work with. It's not every day that your first editor is cut from the same cloth of humor as you *and* helps shape your story in such a real and honoring way. We count ourselves blessed to have been worthy to at least once get a glimpse behind the glossy Zoom photo on our early Zoom calls! Heh heh.

Sarah Atkinson, Vice President and Publisher, who wins every note-taking award that may or may not exist, we knew from the first time we sat down with you and Kara over tacos and margs that we were gonna love working with you. Thank you for coming to Denver to hang out with us, for not being scared off by our . . . well, us-ness, and for helping that Denver day back in March 2022 live on through such intentional notes. Your diligence in this huge task helped us shape the bones of our book, and we couldn't have done this without you.

Stephanie Rische, Senior Editor, thank you for geeking out with us, sitting with us through our next round of edits, and honoring our story with your insightfulness and refinement. The way you painted the walls and decorated our book with us while treating our message as sacred will stick with us. Thank you for advocating for our individual voices and perspectives, at times even to us. The Lord has truly gifted you with loving your authors well through your God-given knack for detail and through your powerful prayers. We don't take either for granted.

Lindsey Bergsma. Ma'am. Listen, you are beyond talented! Thank you for working with us to allow our art and ourselves to be part of our cover. You handled each and every detail with the kind of care meant for the greats. We're so honored that we got to team up with you to put forward a book cover and design that we truly love and can hardly get enough of. We are huge fans of you and your work!

To Rachelle Gardner, thank you for being a great advocate for us through this process. Before your influence, we were a bit lost. You helped us understand this process, and we are so grateful to have you as part of this project with us.

To our current and past counselors and therapists, thank you for proving correct the fact that EVERYONE SHOULD GO TO THERAPY. Thank you for helping us process and grow individually and together.

Lastly, and most importantly, we give glory to God. Thank You, Jesus, for refining us and drawing us nearer to You through this entire process. We are so grateful that You have given us an opportunity to let our wounds glorify Your Great Name. Forever and always: not our will, but Yours be done.

ABOUT THE AUTHORS

Chad and Adaeze Brinkman are a married couple who intention-ally live out their passion of sharing the gospel of Jesus together in their community. Adaeze works in the creative arts and Chad is a physical therapist. They love traveling and adventuring together, taking in the beauty of God's creation and encouraging others to do the same.